LinkedIn Made Easy:
Business Social Networking Simplified

By

Linda Parkinson-Hardman

COPYRIGHT NOTICE

Contents

PRAISE FOR LINKEDIN MADE EASY 2ND EDITION

"Writing this review has made me revisit some of the brilliantly clear information Linda Parkinson-Hardman shares in LinkedIn Made Easy. It is heaven-sent for someone who is just getting started. Yet just as good to pick up and work through if you're a veteran online social networker." Laura McHarrie, Business Advisor, The Hidden Edge, www.thehiddenedge.com

"I'm fairly experienced with LinkedIn, but there were a lot of small details in the book I hadn't used on LinkedIn. LinkedIn is easy enough to just log in and get going, but the strength of the book is how it takes all the disparate elements of LinkedIn and structures them into a sequence of insights and to do's. It's worth buying even for relatively advanced users." Nicholas Garner, CEO, Searchworks, www.searchworks.eu

"The perfect book for anyone wishing to use LinkedIn properly. Lots of tips on how to build the most effective profile, and also what NOT to do (which actually turns out to be quite important in some instances!). I have recommended this book to friends who I know are on LinkedIn but not using it effectively." Tracy Grinter, Outsourced Office. linkedin.com/in/traceygrinter

"This book has been invaluable to me as a new recruit to LinkedIn. I needed something easy-to-follow and written in plain English as I don't have a lot of time to wade through textbooks and this ticked all the boxes... I am recommending it to everyone I meet! Excellent." Liz Gordon, Managing Director, Brilliant Fish PR & Marketing, www.brilliantfish.co.uk

"I read and worked through Linda's book 'LinkedIn Made Easy' and would recommend it to anyone who wants to improve the way they network on LinkedIn. The book is easy to follow. The information is clear and relevant, and hugely helpful." Sui Anukka, www.suianukka.com

"Although I had a LinkedIn profile prior to purchasing this book, I found this book extremely insightful with its handy tips to build and strengthen your

profile. With the increasing use of social media, this book is a step by step guide to help get the best out of LinkedIn both from a personal and professional standpoint." Feyi Omola, International Marketing and Events Manager, International House World Organisation.

"*The book is easy to read and understand, and very useful to a LinkedIn novice. Even for the more experienced user there are still a few gems to be discovered. After all, there is a difference between knowing a programme or social medium and getting the most out of it.*" Marco van den Heuvel, Clinical Research Associate, PAREXEL.

"*Just finished reading "LinkedIn Made Easy" by Linda, what a great read and for me it is going to help me maximise the 250 contacts I have that were just sat gathering idust. The book also helps you set goals and carry out activities, which works for me.*" Marco Tomat, Technical Project Manager, Blue Chip Data Systems, www.bluechip.uk.com

ACKNOWLEDGEMENTS

The success of the original edition of LinkedIn Made Easy was pleasantly unexpected. Encouragement from many sources meant I was able to produce the second edition of the printed book in record time. The on-going support of my extended network, their encouragement and feedback has meant there was always going to be a third edition, it was just a matter of when I would update.

There are some people without whom though this particularly version wouldn't have come about so soon into 2013; they include the amazing Laura McHarrie, who has been a strong advocate since I met her just five years ago. Her constant enthusiasm has been infectious and sustaining and I cannot imagine coming to this project without it. She also gave me the impetus to complete the third edition by telling me she needed it, thanks Laura.

There are so many other people along the way who have shared the journey from PDF ebook sold to raise money for charity to this, the third edition. Some though have stood out in their on-going support and, in no particular order, I'd like to say a huge thank you to David, Joanna, Steve, Dave, Liz, Tamara, Margaret, Anne and Stephen.

I also want to say thanks to my mum, Pat and my sister, Beth. Both of whom encourage me, and believe I can be whatever and whomever I want to be.

Finally, if it weren't for the lovely Stevie, I wouldn't be in the position I am today and so I wouldn't have the opportunity to write. Your on-going encouragement, love and support have helped me enormously; I am so grateful, I love you and thank you from the very bottom of my heart.

PREFACE

Since the original version of this book was completed in 2009, the social networking scene has changed significantly. Perhaps the biggest of all these changes has been the increasing homogenisation of the biggest networks. The ability to 'like', 'share' and 'comment' upon the ubiquitous status update cuts across every single one, often giving the impression to newcomers to the networks that they are all the same, and therefore the same rules apply.

Never has it been so easy to recommend both content and people to those we are connected to. The downside to this constant influx of information is that levels of information overload have increased exponentially.

As a result of these two factors combining, attention levels are dropping and there is a blurring between the professional and social boundaries. I find I'm beginning to see large numbers of people engaging in what can only be described as 'happy clicking', where users run down a list of people or updates clicking 'like' or 'connect', with little awareness of what they are recommending or who will be the (un)lucky recipient of their request. It seems more is still seen as better when the reality is it's discernment that really brings tangible results.

Consequently, the need for a robust strategy determining just what you will be saying, and to whom, has become even stronger. Without one, there is a very real danger of social media burn-out or even rejection by staff and business owners, who feel they are disenfranchised either through lack of understanding, knowledge or even access.

It is into this new reality the third edition of LinkedIn Made Easy is born, and I hope it will continue to empower, educate and inform both new and existing users of LinkedIn.

Updates to the third edition have been made once again due to the ever changing nature of this particular network. No doubt, more changes will come later in the year as they tweak and twiddle to make the network even more effective for users.

INTRODUCTION

According to Jeff Weiner, CEO of LinkedIn, their goal is to develop the world's first economic graph. They are aiming to map the digital footprint of the global economy by identifying the connections that exist between individuals, companies, skills, jobs and professional knowledge. In the long term, they expect this will enable them to spot trending economic opportunities in real time[1]. It's a big vision, and one which they are well on the way to achieving, especially with the latest rounds of updates to the LinkedIn network infrastructure.

With over 225 million users worldwide representing around 125 different professions in 200 countries, LinkedIn is the online social network that seeks to connect people in their professional capacity. By the end of the third quarter in 2012 it was acquiring two new members every second and 64% of members are based outside the United States. It is very different from many other social networks you may already have heard about, such as Facebook, because it focuses on our working lives rather than on our social lives.

One way of looking at it is as an extension of the face to face networking you may do in your local area when you get together with other business people. However, this is networking on a grand scale – how so you might ask?

Well, LinkedIn allows you to connect to a network of people in three ways. Your first degree connections are people you are directly connected to and they are the centre of your network. Each person connected to one of your direct connections is a second degree connection; those who are linked to you through this second level make up your third degree connections.

It uses what we could term, 'friend of a friend' psychology. In other words, I'll recommend this person to you because I know them and have a relationship with them; we value and respect such recommendations far more than others, because there is strong trust element to them.

LinkedIn enables you to find people you have been (or are currently) associated with in a working, business or education environment. The power of such a network lies in the fact it is the people you already know who will probably be best placed to help you do things like:

- Get a new job.

- Find out about prospective employees/employers.

- Research business questions and issues you may have.

- Provide you with networking opportunities you might not have access to otherwise.

- Showcase your expertise, knowledge and skills.

This 'How To' book is designed to get you started using LinkedIn to help you grow and market both yourself and your business. It will help you to:

- Set up an account, if you haven't done so already.

- Create or rewrite your profile so you stand out from the crowd.

- Use it as an effective business networking tool.

- Identify the most appropriate way to use LinkedIn to meet your particular needs.

- Work through the fundamentals of designing a strategy for a personal brand or business.

- Show you how to use the power of the network to grow a business.

- Learn how to connect with the people best placed to help you.

In short, it will give you a head start over the vast majority of users who simply use LinkedIn as a place to post an out of date, inappropriate and pointless CV and gather a sackful of dusty contacts.

LinkedIn offers both free and paid for accounts. The biggest difference between the two is with a paid account you can send InMails to other users you aren't connected; this can be a great way to reach people not in your network.

However, you don't need a paid account to make the most of LinkedIn and there are many ways to expand your network, some of which we'll explore in this book.

CHAPTER 1 - YOUR BUSINESS STRATEGY

Before you get started using LinkedIn it's a good idea to have a strategy of some description. Yes, I know, you'd really like to get stuck in connecting with people, improving your profile, demonstrating your many talents and generally throwing some, not so sticky, mud at walls, hoping it won't slide off before it has a chance to make an impact.

And that's exactly what it will be like if you get started without some idea about what you are trying to achieve. If you don't plan, all you do is add another job to the 'to do' list that doesn't provide much in the way of satisfaction or benefit.

Every good business strategy starts with an objective, and using LinkedIn is no different. In fact, if you don't start with an objective then you'll risk wasting time you don't have on activities that bear little fruit. However, I have lost count of the number of people (and businesses) I have come across over the years who aren't even really sure what their business does, let alone what its objectives are. I don't mean in the 'we make widgets' or 'we are accountants' sense, I mean in the 'we make others people's lives easier' sense.

Identifying what your business does for a person or organisation is the key to identifying appropriate objectives.

Let's say you are a firm of accountants specialising in the SME (small and medium sized enterprise) market. What is the one statement you might make to cause someone in that market sector to take notice of you? It might be something as simple as *'fixed monthly fee for freelancers, sole traders and SME's'*. Why does this matter? Because often they are on tight budgets and it helps to know exactly what is being paid out every month.

Most people buy something whether it's a tin of beans, a complex IT system or a consultant, to solve a problem. And the vast majority of these buying decisions are emotionally driven, even at a corporate level. This applies to everything from which supermarket we use, to the cars we have in the fleet. Everything people do reflects who they think they are and believe themselves to be; it is a reflection of their personality. Even large organisations have personalities.

The needs can be split down as follows:

Emotional need. Some people go shopping to escape from bad moods, others buy brands to attract attention; a third group buys expensive cars to improve their perceived status, while a fourth group might buy certain clothes to appeal to a potential mate.

Being Someone Else. It's a well known phenomenon that we are encouraged to buy brands after seeing 'cool' people in adverts. We want to be like them because we unconsciously associate certain perceived traits or personality types with the brand. If this trait or personality type appeals to us then we'll buy the brand, believing (unconsciously) this action will bring us closer to our perceived ideal state of being.

Follow the Crowd. According to social proof theory[2], things become more appealing when they are desired by others. This allows people and organisations to buy products they don't need just because of their perceived attractiveness. You could say much of the attraction of social media is driven by the perception that we are 'missing out' in some way.

We like the seller. Research consistently shows we prefer to shop from those who smile. This might mean a bad tempered employee or sour faced business person might actually drive clients and customers away

Means to reach their goals. The person who buys a Ferrari might do so in order to attract a potential partner; the woman who buys lingerie might do so to spice up her sex life and, the business person who buys an iPhone may well want to look good in meetings.

Once you have an understanding about why people and companies might buy from you, then you can begin to work on getting their attention. This is the basis of your future strategy and the first action is to set a goal for yourself or your business.

In our fictional accountancy practice this might look something like *'increase the number of monthly billed clients to twenty'*. It's best to be specific with objectives because they can then be tracked and your activities to achieve them can also be measured.

Your objective can probably be broken down into several different goals, each consisting of several elements; for instance your objective to increase billed monthly clients may include a goal of making specific connections with individuals and companies; another might be the amount of business you want to transact; and finally you may have a goal of raising your profile and your perceived levels of expertise amongst both potential customers and your peers.

Bear in mind though, some goals sitting within an overall objective may not be achievable directly through LinkedIn. An example might be if you sell widgets to consumers; as LinkedIn is not a consumer focused platform you will need to think of alternative ways to help you meet the goals necessary to achieve your overall objective. For instance, you might use it to find all the intermediaries who could help you sell widgets to their customers, or you might be able to find a website designer who can help you sell them online.

Each objective you have and it's component goals may rely on working with any one of the five broad groups of stakeholders, these are:

1. Current and future customers (those not running their own business, can substitute employers here).

2. People who have a direct financial interest in the business for instance staff, directors, shareholders and trustees.

3. Your suppliers. For instance you might want to find cheaper suppliers to improve profitability

4. Your competitors. Perhaps by undertaking competitive intelligence research, networking amongst your peers or becoming a recognised industry expert

5. Intermediaries who are the people who can put you in front of your future customers because of what they do or who they are. They might be networkers solely or they may have a related business or industry.

Members of these groups will 'buy', in the loosest sense of the word, from you for different reasons; you can be sure though, those reasons will be to their benefit as much as yours. For example, a particular intermediary may choose to recommend you to his clients because having you to suggest makes him look good or he'll receive a hefty commission from you for each new client.

Each of your products and services may also relate to one or more of these five 'stakeholder' groups. Let's take a simple objective such as increasing profitability. There are several ways you might be able to achieve this. For instance you could:

- Increase the number of products and/or services you sell.

- Increase your prices.

- Reduce the cost of running your business.

Each stakeholder group could help you to achieve these outcomes in one or more different ways. For example, the customer buys a product or service; having the right staff in place will mean greater efficiency; the right suppliers will deliver the right goods on time and within an acceptable price range; keeping in touch with competitors could highlight new opportunities you hadn't thought of and intermediaries can help you to do all three, simply because they know the people and companies you don't, yet!

Setting an objective is often one of the hardest things to do when you are planning any sort of marketing and to be honest most people and businesses rarely do it. They rely on the CV sent out speculatively, the advert they place in the local paper, the listing in a supplier's directory or the recommendations of their current clients. They hope someone will miraculously see they are better than their competitors by osmosis; they don't actively promote themselves, their product or their business. It is true, each of these actions can drive business and change, but they are only a tiny fraction of what you can achieve when you start to think strategically.

Often the reason most of us don't do anything more than taking these reactive actions is because it is perceived as 'selling', and selling is not something a professional feels they should be seen doing. So they sit and wait for business and opportunities to come to them.

According to Ford Harding in his book Rainmaking[3], if you are a professional selling a service, whether that's you or your business, then you can't avoid 'selling' as a fundamental part of your working activity, especially in a difficult economic climate. Selling is, of course, what makes your business or career successful and it's what pays the wages too.

The typical sales process has five basic stages to it:

1. Be seen by those who are actively seeking your services.

2. Identify opportunities and leads.

3. Follow up leads and opportunities.

4. Get a meeting or send a pitch.

5. Close the sale.

Of course, there are many shades of grey in this oversimplified model, and its purpose is simply to highlight the actions you need to take. The reason for mentioning it is networking (whether on or off-line) can help you do the first three of these activities reasonably easily, and it will also help you to build better business relationships too.

Ford Harding also tells us there are five specific things you can do to facilitate all the stages of selling; they are article writing, public speaking, seminars, publicity and networking. You can do all of these things online, albeit not usually in the conventional sense.

LinkedIn gives you the opportunity to show your presentations on your profile, speak publically through group discussions, publicise yourself and your business through status updates, demonstrate your expertise by answering questions and build a network of trusted professionals who know what you do and why you do it well. The only thing it can't do is give you the opportunity to present to an audience in person; however it does allow you to promote any event you are speaking at to get the proverbial 'bums on seats'.

Each of these activities could get you to stage four of the sales process, getting a meeting or sending a proposal/pitch; after that it's up to you to close the sale.

WHY USE LINKEDIN OVER ANY OTHER NETWORK?

There are many social networks, each catering to a different audience and need. That doesn't mean to say you can belong to only one, in fact I belong to several and use each of them for business purposes. It's just the way I use them differs significantly; this is because they each have their own unique environment, personality and audience with rules about what is, and isn't acceptable.

I use LinkedIn, Facebook, Twitter and Google+ on a daily basis; however, at the risk of sounding a little schizophrenic, I am a different person in each and I respond and react to different stimuli from them. What attracts me to pay attention on Facebook doesn't have the same effect on Twitter and vice versa. In other words, I filter out the messages, both obvious and subliminal, that aren't a reflection of the person I am when I'm interacting with a particular audience.

Knowing this, means I craft my own messages specifically for each audience on each network. I know different groups of stakeholders are in different networks; for instance my customers may be on Facebook and my intermediaries could use LinkedIn. Given they are interested in different aspects of what I can provide them they need to see different sides of my knowledge, skill and abilities. This applies equally to a business as well, as you'll see when we get further into this book.

Personally, I prefer LinkedIn to many of the other networks for the simple reason it is more professional. It also happens to be very easy to use and, with a few simple tricks and actions, you can make it work more effectively in your favour.

I mentioned a few reasons to use LinkedIn in the introduction; I've included a fuller list here, just to get you thinking:

- Write recommendations for people you know, whose work you have valued.

- Display recommendations received from people who like your work.

- Demonstrate your expertise by sharing presentations on your profile.

- Give people access to your unique information and perspective through downloads and presentations.

- List any jobs you have to the whole community.

- Find out who is recruiting and research companies before you apply.

- Find recommended contractors and product/service providers by asking your network.

- Use polls for quick and simple market research.

- Answer questions and take part in discussions demonstrating your expertise without a hint of self-promotion.

- Take part in industry and market specific discussions.

- Publish your own, unique LinkedIn web address on all of your marketing literature.

- Use your status updates as a way to showcase your current list of projects.

- Use status updates to share information, articles and resources with your network.

- Connect with like-minded fellows who share common passions and aims.

- Keep an eye on companies you would like to work with in the future.

- Follow the latest business news and updates from people you admire.

Mostly, the list of things above that you can use LinkedIn for falls into one of four camps:

1. Marketing -- your business, products, services or even yourself.

2. Research – market or professional development.

3. Personal Brand Building – to create a dynamic, visible profile as an expert or specialist.

4. Support – for customers, your peers and your network.

However, what you may have felt when presented with the list above is something along the lines of, *"what, you want me to do all that, when am I going to find the time and how am I going to do it?"*

The trick is to start with your overall objective as we discussed at the beginning of this chapter; then choose one of the four camps listed above and finally, decide on your first goal. For instance, you might be like our fictional accountant who is looking to increase profitability. One goal might be to find some alternative suppliers to reduce your costs. The camp you may put yourself in would probably be research. In this way, you have now narrowed down the focus of your initial activity on LinkedIn. You will have reduced the fear, increased your focus and begun to identify the actions you can take which will be most effective in helping to reduce costs.

Now is the time to start employing some blue sky thinking and perhaps get the help of your colleagues, employees and friends. The process of identifying how to work with an objective is as follows:

1. Establish the specific goals that will ensure you achieve your objective. Make them smart (specific, measurable, achievable, realistic and time bound). They must be something which can be measured, rather than a woolly statement meaning nothing.

2. Ask everyone to contribute ideas about how each goal can be achieved without discussion or criticism as you don't know at this stage just what might be effective.

3. Group the ideas for each goal into categories and then discuss which ones are realistic. For instance, saying that talking to your Head of State about a problem might not be realistic; sending a letter to the appropriate Government Minister just might.

4. Each goal now has a set of realistic actions you can take, each action taken contributes to achieving the goal, and each goal achieved contributes to your overall objective.

5. Give someone (assuming you have more than one person available to you) the responsibility of managing each action, with one person coordinating effort towards a specific goal. If you are

doing this alone, then my suggestion would be to start with the goal and set of actions most likely to have the broadest reach.

Let's take an objective like increasing the number of SME clients you have by twenty. Your first goal might be to improve your networking skills. Therefore the actions you could take would probably include:

- Talking to your current clients about the service you provide to find out why they think you are the best thing since sliced bread.

- Asking for testimonials about the service you provide to share on your profile, company profile and website.

- Breaking the comments down into sales hooks that capture people's attention and use these as status updates.

- Committing to networking both on and off-line to build up your profile.

- Getting a better understanding of the factors affecting SME's currently.

- Asking your current clients if they would introduce you to one business or person they feel you might be able to help.

Your overall objective can be broken down into smaller and smaller elements; each one is more easily achieved because it requires less input and work, but collectively they have a great impact. There is truth in saying *'the whole is greater than the sum of the parts'*.

Below, I've created a list of a few actions you might decide to take on LinkedIn if you were to have a goal such as committing to networking.

1. Add the people you already work with to your network.

2. Have a look at who people in your current network might be able to introduce you to.

3. Use the search facility on LinkedIn to find others with the same, or complimentary skills; send them a message asking them if they would be interested in connecting.

4. Read people's profiles and watch their online activities to determine whether they know what they are talking about.

5. Find two groups which reflect the market sector you work in and see if there are discussions taking place you can get involved in.

6. Start a discussion on one of the groups yourself about the area you are interested in and respond to replies and comments. Asking a question like *"can anyone recommend a person in this field?"* or *"how can I develop a particular service further?"* could be good starting points.

7. Tell your network about products and services you need in your status updates.

8. Use your summary to explain your own services, skills and knowledge using industry keywords so you show up in search results across LinkedIn.

9. Follow the updates of people and companies you respect and admire.

10. Share, comment on and 'like' helpful information and content others have provided.

These simple steps will enable you to find out what is needed, the information people value and what your current network members think about in just one single social network. Imagine if that were replicated across multiple social and face-to-face networks. And, I'll bet it doesn't feel like selling either.

It is worth bearing in mind that every single action you take will also stand alone quite happily; you don't have to do all of them or even some of them. Just one of them could be enough to get you to stage four of the sales process. But, as in life, the more you can do the better, because you are giving yourself the best possible chance of being 'seen' by the right person, at the right time in accordance with the objective you've already set yourself and the specific goals you have set to meet this objective.

Chapter 13 contains a number of simple 'recipes' you could follow for a variety of different objectives and situations.

If you have an account you can skip the next chapter, although it might be helpful to review the information if you are still relatively new to the network. If you don't, this is where you get started.

CHAPTER 2 - CREATING A LINKEDIN ACCOUNT

Creating an account on LinkedIn is relatively straightforward and starts at the LinkedIn home page. You can find the network by typing *www.linkedin.com* into your preferred web browser.

Step 1

Once you have added your First Name, Last Name, Email Address and your chosen Password (you can create a strong password by including upper and lowercase letters, numbers and symbols) and clicked on the *Join Now* button you will be redirected to a page that asks you whether you are employed, a business owner, working independently, looking for work or a student. You need to pick the one which matches your *current state* most accurately.

Step 2

Complete the answers to the questions you are presented with, these will be dependent on the status you gave yourself in Step 1.

Step 3

Now you can import the email addresses of your current contacts if you use one of the following services: Yahoo!, Gmail, AOL or Hotmail. If you choose to do this, and *I suggest you don't*, you will need to share your username and password for these accounts with LinkedIn so it can retrieve the information it needs to work with.

Timely Warning: Connecting your LinkedIn account to an email account could blast an email to every one of your contacts with the message 'I'd like to add you to my professional network'. If it does, you probably won't even know who the message has been sent to until you start getting emails asking 'why' or finding your mother is commenting on your updates. Although you can link the two, the question has to be why would you want to?

In Chapter 5, we'll be looking at the right way to build a valuable network, made up of people who could benefit you, rather than having a huge network filled with people who don't even remember your name, never mind what you do.

Step 4

Finally, you need to confirm your identity by proving your email address is genuine. This is common practice online, and is just one of the ways in which organisations try to filter out spam and malicious users.

You'll receive an email containing a sentence saying "click here to confirm your email address". Just click the link or copy the full web address given into your web browser.

This confirms to LinkedIn your email address is genuine and not just a robot trying to create false (spam) accounts.

Once you have clicked, you will be asked to confirm it's you by logging in with the email address you used and your new password - you did remember to write it down, didn't you?

And that's it; your account at LinkedIn is created. Now all you have to do is use it correctly, and that's the subject for the rest of the book.

CHAPTER 3 - GETTING STARTED

The first time you login to LinkedIn, you'll be presented with a 'build your network box' that suggests you start using your current contacts; it's very similar to the questions that were being asked when you first signed up.

It's no wiser now than it was when you signed up to connect your email account to your LinkedIn account; after all you want to exercise control over the people you invite to be connections, not just add everyone you have ever emailed to a list.

It is worth remembering the reason LinkedIn would like you to connect your two accounts is because their aim is to increase the number of users; after all large user numbers look good to LinkedIn shareholders and investors.

From now on, whenever you login to LinkedIn you will always start on your home page. Your home page is unique to your account, so you will only see the things that are happening with your network and the people or companies you follow. As you scroll down the page you will see it is divided into two halves:

Left-hand side

At the top is a box where you can add a status update; underneath this is a self-updating section pulling in the latest news updates from LinkedIn Today.

The rest of the left-hand side is made up of a stream of the most recent updates from everyone in your personal network; these are displayed chronologically with the most recent at the top. You can filter this stream by using the drop-down menu to show the '*Top*' (most popular) and '*All*' updates; personally, I keep it set to '*All*' as I want to see what the whole of my network is doing. As you scroll down the page you will find more items load automatically.

The advantage of having a home page that displays in this way is it allows you to see at a glance what the most recent activity is. Giving you a quick overview of what's hot and what's trending.

Right-hand side

The right-hand side of your home page shows a mixture of different things. A box showing the photo's and names of *People You May Know* is automatically generated by LinkedIn according to other people in your network. The assumption is if you are connected to X then you probably also know Y; of course real life doesn't work like this, but sometimes it can make useful suggestions. This section changes randomly every time you load this page.

Ad's you may be interested in is a series of adverts from other users of LinkedIn.

The *Who's Viewed Your Profile* section gives you a quick overview of the numbers of people who have viewed your profile and how frequently you show up in search results.

If you click on the link to *See More*, you'll be taken to a page where you will find a list of the viewers; sometimes these will be specific people, others will be generic. Which you see for any given profile visitor is dependent on the settings they have chosen to use (you can find out more about this in the section on *Profile Settings* later in this chapter. To get the most accurate and insightful information for either of these statistics, you will need to have a paid account.

Your LinkedIn Network shows the basic statistics for your particular network of connections right out to the third level. The link will take you to a list of your first level connections; this page has a useful set of filters you can apply from the left-hand side and at the top of the list. It can make very interesting reading.

The link to the total number of network members will take you to a set of LinkedIn search results you can filter by degree of separation from you; first degree, second degree or third degree connections.

Groups You May Like is a randomly generated list of LinkedIn Groups you aren't yet a member of; it is probably based on a mix of the keywords in your profile and the groups you are currently a member of.

Companies You May Wish To Follow is also randomly generated based on your profile, the companies you already follow and the industry sector you placed yourself in during the sign-up process.

With each section, you get the opportunity to 'see more' suggestions.

NAVIGATING AROUND LINKEDIN

Navigating around LinkedIn can be a frustrating experience for the new user. Basically it falls into three 'menu' areas.

The first menu area sits right at the top of every page. It includes the LinkedIn icon and clicking this will return you to your LinkedIn home page. You will also find the search box with a drop down menu allowing you to choose the section on the left hand side. Clicking 'advanced' takes you to an advanced search page with many more options available to you.

Next in the line are three notification icons, the first is flags new messages you've received and you can hover over each one shown to take an action such as reply. The second icon allows you to see a list of notifications about actions taken on your account including endorsements and profile views. Try not to click the names because you'll only be taken to your own profile in edit mode. The third icon is allows you to add connections by connecting your LinkedIn account to your email account.

Finally, this particular menu is completed by a little image of you. Hovering over this image allows you to get to various parts of your LinkedIn account quickly and easily. It also provides a quick and simple way to access the LinkedIn Help Center.

The second menu sits immediately underneath the first and contains links to the following parts of LinkedIn:

- Home Page
- Your Profile
- Your Network
- Jobs being advertised on LinkedIn
- Your Interests

Some of these links have sub links that appear when you hover them. Why not try them out and see where they go?

On the far right hand side of this menu you will find premium options and an upgrade link. This will take to you sections of the LinkedIn system which require payment to use.

The third menu can be found at the bottom of every page. It's worth not trying to use it from the home page as this has an infinity scroll on it that automatically loads updates when you scroll to the bottom.

When you do get it though you'll find links to functional parts of LinkedIn which allow you to find out more about LinkedIn itself as well links to the as user and privacy agreements you signed up to when you joined.

SETTING THE SETTINGS

The settings function on LinkedIn controls what the vast majority of people, both on and off the network, can see. It also helps to control what activities you are alerted to and which ones you ignore.

Some of the settings specifically for groups will be covered in Chapter 7. In this chapter we will be concerning ourselves only with what you might want other people to see about you and your activity.

Your settings can be controlled from a variety of locations. The easiest way to access the Settings Dashboard is by using the drop-down menu you can find under your profile picture in the top right-hand corner of every page. From here you can access and control everything, including what people logged into LinkedIn can see, as well as what can be indexed by external search engines such as Google.

Sometimes you may be prompted to update your settings when you take certain actions across the LinkedIn network, this will automatically load the Settings Dashboard.

It is also important to know that every time you choose to access the settings part of your account you will be prompted to put in your password. This is a security measure that can help to prevent problems from occurring in your account.

WHY DO I NEED TO CONTROL MY SETTINGS?

A good example of having rigid settings that prevent indexing by search engines and random viewing is the person looking for employment who doesn't want their current employer to know.

However, the vast majority of users of LinkedIn will be actively seeking to promote themselves, their business and/or their career. Therefore being aware about what you could, and should, change is always well worth it.

The settings dashboard is split into two areas; the first allows you to upgrade and manage your account on LinkedIn; the second allows you to manage the settings associated with the following four areas:

- Your profile.

- Your email preferences.

- Your groups, companies and applications.

- Your account.

Clicking on each of these sections will show you the various elements you can affect through settings.

PRIVACY

In 2011, Linkedin introduced a new default setting associated with what is called 'social advertising'. Whenever you take an action on LinkedIn that involves following a company or recommending people or services, LinkedIn may use this 'knowledge' to pick the most relevant adverts to show you and others on the network; it may also use your name and photograph next to relevant adverts both on LinkedIn and in other websites too. This is turned on by default.

Therefore, you need to review what you are happy for LinkedIn to use your data in connection with.

To turn off seeing adverts from LinkedIn on other websites you visit you will need to click on *Account* in the Settings Dashboard. Select *Manage Advertising Preferences* and un-tick the box next to '*LinkedIn may show me ads on third party websites*'.

To turn off the use of your data in adverts on LinkedIn, click on Groups, Companies and Applications; select *Turn on/off Data Sharing with Third Party Applications*, and un-tick the box.

To turn off the use of your data in LinkedIn plugins on third-party websites (websites other than LinkedIn) you will click on *Groups, Companies and Applications*, select *Manage Settings for LinkedIn Plugins on Third Party Sites*, and un-tick the box.

Each of these actions will remove your picture and name from appearing in LinkedIn specific adverts across the web.

YOUR PUBLIC PROFILE

This is the place most people will want to start when it comes to knowing what others might see, or have access to, as these are the settings which determine what people (and search engines like Yahoo!, Bing and Google) outside the LinkedIn network can see.

You can find the settings for your *Public Profile* under the *Account* tab on the Settings Dashboard. When you click on the link to *Edit Your Public Profile*, you are presented with two options; the first is to customise your public profile, the second is to change your public profile URL.

I have assumed in this book that the vast majority of readers will be keen to use LinkedIn as a way of promoting themselves or their business, and if this is the case you will need to select *Make My Profile Visible to Everyone*. You can turn off individual elements but to be honest if you don't want to be seen online then you probably shouldn't be using social networks.

Now your profile is visible it can be indexed by the search engines. This increases the chance anyone looking for you through the likes of Bing, Yahoo! and Google will be able to find your LinkedIn profile at the top of any set of search results.

Now, let's say you haven't really completed your profile yet. You may not want to show parts of it to the wider world and those can be easily turned off simply by un-ticking the relevant box. Just remember to turn it back on again when you've finished your editing.

You can see exactly what will be displayed on the left-hand side of the same screen view. This gives you the chance to check you are happy with what is showing.

YOUR PUBLIC PROFILE URL

When you create your LinkedIn account you will be given a unique web address, you can find it at the end of the *Contact Info* section of your profile. Others can click on this or be given it to view your public profile.

It will probably contain your name and a few random characters, and you have the chance to change it to something more memorable in this section of the settings dashboard.

To change it, all you need to do is click on *Customize your Public Profile URL* give yourself a new moniker in the box you are presented with. Clicking *Set Custom URL* will update it for you and everyone else too.

Mine is *www.linkedin.com/in/lindaph*; if you type this into a web-browser you'll see my public profile and from there you can login to LinkedIn to see more. The one you can use will depend on what others on the network have already claimed, so you may need to play around with a few alternatives before settling on one. Remember, you can change it at any time you want; although, if you do decide to use your public profile address on business cards, you may want to avoid changing it in the future.

GENERAL SETTINGS

It's now time to set and manage the general settings for your LinkedIn account. You can find all of the relevant links from the Settings Dashboard. This page gives you lots of options to check and uncheck at will. From here you can determine things like whether others can see your contacts, if you want to participate in market research surveys, who can find your profile in the network and the type of contact you're happy to receive from people you don't yet know.

It's also here you would go if you decided to close your LinkedIn account, or if you accidentally added multiple email addresses.

PROFILE SETTINGS

The profile settings give you an opportunity to edit your profile, as well as access various settings such as managing the recommendations you receive, controlling which actions you take are broadcast to your network, set who can see your connections, control your member feed and any Twitter accounts you may have.

Your *member feed* is what governs the information and activities that appear on other people's home pages. I have mine set to *everyone*, because I want the widest possible exposure for my LinkedIn actions as I'm using the network to promote both myself and my business.

You can add as many Twitter accounts as you have, I have included just my main account @lindaph as this is the one I use the most frequently. If you choose to add more, only one will be your primary account and this is the one you would send LinkedIn status updates to Twitter from, if it were turned on.

In the majority of cases, because you are probably using LinkedIn to promote yourself, you will want to set your visibility to the widest possible setting of everyone. The exception to this might be who can see your connections. I have mine set so they are visible to just my first level connections; you will need to take a view on this as it may be affected by the industry you work in, who your connections are and whether they require privacy or not.

This section is also where you can control whether other people will know if you have visited their profile. Remember, in Chapter 3 where we saw the '*Who's Viewed My Profile*' tab on our home page? Well this is how people control what can be seen. Personally, I'm quite happy for people to know I've visited them, but you may have a good reason not to do so.

EMAIL NOTIFICATIONS

Do you want to receive email from the people connected to you and from those who might like to contact you? I'd be surprised if the answer were 'no', after all this is a networking opportunity where the objective is to meet people and do business.

You may though have a perfectly good reason why you don't want the world and his wife contacting you; it is in this section of settings you can control what does and doesn't happen.

This is also where you can turn off emails coming from advertisers on the LinkedIn network, these are called *Partner InMails*.

GROUPS, COMPANIES AND APPLICATION SETTINGS

This is the section which allows you to manage the companies you follow, how you receive email from groups and how applications interact with your personal data.

ACCOUNT SETTINGS

From here you can change your password and email address; you can customise the information shown on your home page, change your language and also whether you connect to LinkedIn over a secure setting (this is the same sort of setting you would connect to your bank with). You can also upgrade or close your account.

You can also choose whether to view LinkedIn updates in an RSS reader. RSS means many different things, but the most popular is Really Simple Syndication. Whenever you (or your network) undertake an action on LinkedIn this can be broadcast to a 'news reader' of your/their choice. This means you don't have to be permanently connected to LinkedIn to find out what's going on in your network.

CHAPTER 4 - BUILD & IMPROVE YOUR PROFILE

Now you have the basic settings under your belt, and you understand more about how LinkedIn both displays, and uses, your data, it is time to start building the perfect profile.

Without doubt, your profile is the most important part of your LinkedIn experience. If your profile isn't complete or accurate then you will be missing out on vital opportunities for you, your business or career. Your profile is the place other people visit to see who you are, what you do and what skills, knowledge and specialities you have.

According to LinkedIn, those who have a complete profile are 40% more likely to receive opportunities too[5]. So it's worth getting it done sooner, rather than later.

As a minimum, a good profile on LinkedIn must include the following elements:

1. A head and shoulders photograph of you in your normal business dress (where appropriate!). Please don't use a cartoon or a logo; LinkedIn is the online equivalent of a business networking meeting and if you wouldn't show up with a bag over your head why do it online.

A good photograph allows users to see you and remember you. People like to see who they are 'talking' to and you'd be surprised at the number of people who remember your name but just can't bring you to mind. By the way remember to smile, research shows that photographs with people smiling get a better response and more engagement than those that don't[3].

2. A headline. This is a short statement of 120 characters telling people more about what you do and how you add value to the world.

Between them, your photograph and headline are the most important elements, this is because they appear in the search results of LinkedIn. A good headline is what can make the difference between someone clicking through to read your profile, or not.

3. A summary of up to 2,000 characters (including spaces). This should be based in the present rather than the past. A good summary is an elevator pitch and it should tell me:

- who you are

- what you do

- why you do it

- what value you add to your customers or clients.

It is *not* designed to tell me what you studied, where you studied or what you did for your last employer unless it is highly relevant to where you are in your career or business now, or whether you are engaged or not.

4. Your contact details. Please don't skimp on these if you are serious about networking online. This is not the time to be shy about sharing your email address or business phone number; after all the purpose of this effort is to put you in the best possible position to grow your personal brand or business.

5. A set of specialities. These are keywords reflecting your knowledge and areas of expertise.

6 A set of skills and expertise. These are keywords representing your skills and expertise. It is important to pick these skills carefully

as this is what others will endorse you for. You'll find more information about endorsements in Chapter 9 on Advanced Profiles.

7. Experience and Past Roles. Your LinkedIn profile is not a CV, but it does have some of the elements of a CV and this is one of them. However, you do not need to add details about everything you have done. The most important elements to concentrate on are those which inform your present. If your current role is Sales Director then demonstrating you were an award winning sales manager would be important and highly relevant; but being a cleaner whilst at University, although worthwhile, isn't.

8. Your education. List your education, concentrating on the highest levels of qualification you have attained. Again, if it's not directly relevant to your current career or your future aspirations, then you can leave it at just School (University/College), Degree, Field of Study and Dates. If, on the other hand, it is directly relevant then you might want to include information about the grade, and a description of the main areas of your course or research.

There is the opportunity to create a more advanced profile that takes you beyond the basics and we will look at this in Chapter 9. For the time being though, creating the basic profile will allow you to begin networking and meeting the objectives you have set yourself.

Before you get started on your new profile it might be worth reviewing the following questions as well as your past positions first. This is because you will have skills, knowledge and experience as relevant today as they were in the past and it is worth highlighting them. After all, you never know why someone will want to connect or work with you and one of these could be the key element.

- What are the elements of the role that are relevant in my current position?

- What goals have I already achieved; my own and employers?

- What are my personal goals now?

- How will my personal goals match my objectives for my business or career?

Here is my list of top tips for writing and updating your profile on LinkedIn:

1. As with any news story, the first thing seen needs to capture people's attention. This needs to describe you in your own voice and telling the reader what makes you stand out from the crowd, is unique or different about the skills, knowledge and experience you have that others in your profession don't. You might also want to mention, if they are relevant, any awards or competitions you have won, whether you were top of your year, or honoured as the best.

2. When you add your website addresses, don't forget to use relevant keywords in the link text, this is for optimisation purposes on the major search engines. The default link text will say 'company website' rather than the company name, the full web address or something more appropriate. To change your website link text to something more relevant, select *Other* from the drop-down list against the type of website instead of one of the other options; this allows you to customise the words used in the link text.

3. Your summary should say who you are and what you do; this is not necessarily the specifics of your job unless your job is highly

technical, but how you add value. Therefore, you wouldn't say "I sell cars"; but you might say "I get people from A to B safely with our 42 point used car test". It is also appropriate to add your personal work related goals in here too.

4. Explain the context of your experience; the vast majority of people won't know what ABC Widgets Ltd do and they probably don't really care, unless it is of direct relevance to them. However, an employer looking for someone to head-hunt will be interested in the person who is best able to meet the needs they have.

5. Explain the context of your education as well if it's relevant to what you are doing now.

6. Use the additional information section you are provided with at the bottom of the profile page. LinkedIn is about people and relationships; therefore show your readers you are, in fact, a real person. But don't go overboard, this isn't Facebook so it doesn't require a warts and all exposé; your connections don't need to know if you are married nor do they need to know when your birthday is.

7. Finally, update your contact settings to let people know what you are interested in. You can do this at the bottom of the profile. Others may not read them, but some do. I also use this as an opportunity to share my contact details again, just in case someone can't see them because of the distance between us in network relationships. At the moment, mine reads

"I'm available to help you implement a social media or Internet marketing strategy. I'm also happy to come along to your event as a keynote speaker or presenter on the subject of Social Media, Social Enterprise and Non-Profit use of the Internet. You can contact me by email at: linda@internet-mentor.co.uk or call me on +44(0)08432892142. However, before you get in touch I'd appreciate it if you could think about, and then let me know:

1. Why you particularly want me to get involved?
2. Why my involvement might help you change your world?
3. How it will meet my aims and objectives and match the things I'm interested in? (see my summary above for the sorts of things that interest me)."

HOW TO EDIT YOUR PROFILE

Each element of your profile can be edited by using the little pen icon that appears next to each section when you are in edit mode. You can select *edit mode* from the drop-down menu under the *Profile* link in the top navigation bar.

You can add additional jobs and educational experiences to your profile by using the plus sign next to the Education and Experience sections. There is just one thing to be aware of if you edit your experience, LinkedIn will prompt you to update your headline with the new title you have just added. You probably don't want to do this if you've spent time perfecting the ideal 120 character description. Chapter 9 goes into much more detail about the advanced elements of your profile; these take you from basic to advanced expert.

Whenever you visit your profile page, LinkedIn may prompt you to add more information and additional sections. It might also ask you questions and offer suggestions and you can choose to answer these, skip the question or close the update prompt box.

CHAPTER 5 - CREATING A CONNECTION STRATEGY

Some of you will already have a number of connections on LinkedIn and others won't have any. However, it is important you determine what your connection strategy going forward is to be otherwise it can be a daunting prospect. Remember you are effectively in a networking room with millions of other people and, the most important thing you need to ask when considering connections is "what am I hoping LinkedIn will do for me?"

The reason we talk about 'me', rather than 'my business', is because LinkedIn, as a social network, is essentially about the individual, reflecting who and what they know. The key to understanding this new world is the word 'social' from social networking as it revolves around building strong, useful and vibrant business and professional relationships.

LinkedIn is a place that allows you to demonstrate your expertise in a given sector of the economy, where you can showcase your projects, talents, knowledge and skills. Your business, if you have one, or the company you work for are a part of who you are, not the whole of who you are.

Therefore, your use of this particular social network should really be about driving attention towards you, the individual who adds value to the world, as well as the businesses and organisations you are a part of, in a set of unique ways.

At the last count, there were over 225 million professionals with a profile on LinkedIn. However, not all of those profiles are current, and not everyone you meet online will be the sort of person you want to connect with.

Have a think about the following questions and see if you can answer them:

1. Would you like to link only with people you know? This is the route recommended by LinkedIn. It's a good policy, at least to begin with, because networking, on or off-line is all about the relationships you develop with the people you know.

2. Are there any actions you can take that facilitate the start of a relationship? I often ask the people who get involved with me in group discussions to connect if it seems we have something in common.

3. Would you be open to connecting with people you don't yet know in the hopes of building a much larger, broader network? Such people are often referred to as LIONS, (LinkedIn Open Networker's). These individuals are prepared to link to people they don't know to open up networks that may be otherwise closed. I do link to people I don't know, but I make sure I check them out first by reading their profile to see if they are an appropriate 'fit'. In other words I'm looking to see if they are interested in the same things I'm interested in, or if they are just trying to get to my network of contacts?

4. Is your business B2B (business focused) or is it B2C (consumer focused)? Knowing which it is will help you to decide which of the five stakeholder groups you would like to focus on and the sort of result you are looking for. It doesn't just have to be clients or employers, it could be equally useful to help you look for collaborations or undertake continuing professional development.

5. Who in your audience uses LinkedIn? For instance, as CEO of The Hysterectomy Association I know if any members are using this social network they probably wouldn't want their work

colleagues making assumptions about their health issues. Therefore, seeking connections with them probably isn't very appropriate. That doesn't mean I'm not connected to members, but it was they who made the connection request.

6. Would you be prepared to link to past or current employers or employees? Think about this one carefully, because they will know things about you which you might not wish to be made public in the present day. Alternatively, they could be your biggest fans.

7. Is it appropriate to link to all your customers, clients and suppliers? After all this is another group full of advocates and allies.

8. What about people you might meet whilst out networking in the physical world? I often send a request to join me on LinkedIn when I have met someone at a business event. This practice also means I don't have to worry about the business cards I collect, as all the information is stored within my LinkedIn Network Dashboard.

Once you have some appropriate answers to the questions above, then it's time to start working on increasing your connections. But first, a few don'ts before you begin putting your strategy into place:

Don't spam – in other words, don't come to LinkedIn hoping to sell your wares. This is a place to network and, although business happens within it, people actually want to focus on developing a relationship with you, not listen to a 'pitch'.

Don't forget who might see your profile – remember some of it may be visible with a very basic search for your name. In fact, why not go along to your favourite search engine and see if you can find yourself; I'll bet your LinkedIn profile comes up pretty high on the list if you've been a member for any length of time.

Don't send out canned invitations – there is a reason why there is a link to *Include a Personal Note* on the main connection page. By writing something personal in the message, people will be more likely to remember you and want to link with you. This is because you are demonstrating you know something about them and therefore appear more interested in them, and not just their list of connections.

Don't preach to the converted – if someone you are asking to become a connection is already listed on LinkedIn, there is no need to tell them about the benefits of being on the site, they already know that and either use it or not.

Don't get upset if people don't accept your invitation – it may be they have their own connection strategy in place that doesn't include the group of people you are in; or it may be they don't want to use the site.

How to Request a Connection

As with many computing and communication skills, there are several ways in which you can request new connections; they are not all equally helpful, but they do all serve the same function.

The fastest and easiest, but least satisfactory in the long term, is to use the *Add Connections* link from the Network Dashboard or the drop down menu under network when you are logged in. By selecting your email provider, you can send an email to all your contacts at once. However, this may blast a standard, canned connection request message which says 'I'd like to add you to my professional network', and you won't know who has actually received it.

The second way is to use the *People You May Know* feature which appears in the right-hand sidebar of your LinkedIn home page. The accounts listed are automatically updated and changed every time this page refreshes; they are chosen because they are already connected to someone you know. When you click on *connect* next to their photograph, you are taken to a main connection page where you are able to define how you know the person and then send them a personalised message, putting your request into context.

What do I mean by putting your request into context? Well, we all meet lots of people throughout the course of our lives and, with the best will in the world; we probably don't remember them all. I don't know about you, but if I attend a networking event I probably speak to a couple of dozen people throughout its course. If they then send me a connection request with no context, then there is every chance I may not even remember who they are. By letting me know we chatted at a particular event and about a specific subject, they give me the chance to bring them to mind again.

The sort of message I might send would be *"It was great to meet you at last nights networking event and I enjoyed our chat about LinkedIn networking. I wonder if you might do me the honour of accepting my connection request. Kindest Regards, Linda PH"*.

Putting it into context like this means they are likely to remember me from the crowd of people they probably talked to. However, you don't have a huge amount of space, roughly four or five lines of text, so keep it simple.

When you are choosing how you know the person you will be presented with a number of options; these are: *Colleague, Classmate, We've done business together, Friend, Other, I don't know XYZ.* Unsurprisingly, if you choose the last option you won't get any further.

You may find some of the options require you to have an email address for the person you are contacting; if you don't have it handy, you may be able to find it on their profile; typically towards the bottom of the page under *Contact Preferences*.

Timely Warning: If you choose the *See More* option available through the *People You May Know* feature, you will be taken to a long list of people with *Connect* next to each one. It is tempting to do 'happy clicking'; scanning down the list clicking connect, connect, connect; however doing so will blast the standard canned connection request message to the (not so) lucky recipients.

In my opinion, the best way to create a potentially meaningful connection is to actually choose to connect with someone before you even open up LinkedIn. You can use the search facility at the top of the page to find their name.

If you end up with a list of possible results, you will notice LinkedIn provides a handy advanced search facility on the left-hand side of the page. This allows you to filter the results by a variety of different factors, including: company details, location, relationships, industry, education and groups. When you are sure you have found the right person, read their profile thoroughly and then use the *Connect* button to bring up the connection page. This allows you to send the, all-important, personalised request.

As you build your network on LinkedIn, you'll be able to check your network statistics regularly to see how you are doing, and to see where the bulk of your network is currently located. You can see this information on your Profile page. Scroll down the page until you see the section on the right-hand side which says *Your Network*. The drop-down menu allows you to change the view by company, school, location, industry and skills. Hovering over the circles in each view shows you unique data specific to your network.

The companion to this data is that which you'll find on other people's profiles; this shows you how their network is made up, as well as how you are connected and what you have in common with them in terms of the skills, locations, companies and schools you have both listed.

Now you understand the fundamentals of connecting, it is important to think through your strategy before taking any action. Answering the following questions should help you clarify your aims and objectives.

1. Would you like to link only with people you know? If so, why?

2. Is your business B2B or is it B2C? Does this matter if your consumer audience are professionals for instance?

3. Who in your audience uses LinkedIn? Are there any things you need to take into account?

4. Would you be prepared to link to past or current employers or employees? If not, why not?

5. Is it appropriate to link to all your customers, clients and suppliers? Are there some you might not want to link to and why?

6. What about people you might meet whilst out networking? What do you already do with their business cards, if anything?

SEARCHING FOR CONNECTIONS

It is worth knowing that sometimes you won't be able to see the full profile of someone you have come across on LinkedIn. The reason for this is that anyone who is in your third level or connections or below (in other words they aren't connected to you at all) are only visible to those who have a paid account.

There is a way round this restriction though. If you copy and paste their name into the search box at the top of LinkedIn pages and then search for them, you will find that when you click their name their full profile becomes visible to you. This is because LinkedIn has to then assume you know them in order to facilitate the process of you connecting.

CHAPTER 6 - MANAGING YOUR CONNECTIONS

How often are you given a business card? Is it daily, weekly, monthly? Do you get them at every networking event you attend, or pick them up from the counter of local suppliers and shops?

I have gathered hundreds over the years and I know people who gather thousands. The sad truth is if someone doesn't do something with a business card they've received straight away, then it will either be consigned to the bin, or a 'storage' facility, destined never to see the light of day again.

Some people have decided the way to manage this information overload is to use a spread-sheet, a contact management system or even Outlook. The problem they find though is they still have to:

- Remember the person they want to speak to so they can find them again.

- Actively do something to keep in touch.

But what if you had a system that kept all your business contacts in one easy to find place, which prompts you every time someone you knew was doing something of interest, and also allows you to share information, or have a conversation, with a single click of the mouse.

LinkedIn offers you a fantastic opportunity to manage all those business details in one easy place, with the added facility of quickly and easily catching up with any of the people you have met over the years. You can find such a system when you click on Network in the top menu bar.

The Network Dashboard provides you with easy access to everything you need to manage the members of your network at the first level. *Contacts* is the first page you come to when you click on the Network Link. This is the place that lists your contacts. You can change the way the list presents by either using the drop down menu on the right hand side or the filters shown on the left. The drop down menu allows you to see people by recent conversation, newly added, alphabetical, company, location or lost touch.

The left hand filters include:-

- Saved (profiles you come across that you choose to save for later).

- Tags (some automatically generated and others you create).

- Companies

- Titles (job titles).

- Locations (with a heat map).

- Sources (from Gmail or Google contacts or Google Calendar).

- Potential Merges (allows you to find people with duplicate accounts).

- Hidden (these are contacts you've uploaded to LinkedIn who don't yet have their own account).

You are also able to see your most recent connections; this is useful as it allows you to quickly follow up by sending a message to them to say 'hello' after your first level connection has been established.

The 'Lost Touch' filter can be a useful prompt, reminding you to send a message or follow up with people you have spoken to in some time.

At the top of the Contacts section you will also see a gear wheel icon, this takes you to the contacts settings for your account. This is where you can export your list of contacts, sync with other accounts you may have online to keep all your contact data in one place.

Each contact provides you with basic information such as their name, their profile photograph and that all-important headline. You will also see any tags you have used to group them and clicking a tag will subdivide your list of contacts into a small sub-set of the whole.

Hovering over the contact will also give you the opportunity to tag your contact with a useful keyword that means something to you. For instance you might use words like 'client' or 'prospect', county or what you have in common.

You can also send them a message, hide them from your contacts list or remove them as a connection altogether.

When you click on their name you will be taken to their profile page and here you'll find a section that allows you to add a note, create a reminder (say for a birthday, meeting or event), how you met (useful for keeping on top of just what has worked with your online marketing and what hasn't) and tags.

If you have your Linkedin account synced to something like your Google or Outlook Calendar then it will also import the dates and times of meetings.

You can also quickly flick to their contact information, giving you easy access to their phone number, email address, business address, website and Twitter accounts. You'll also see icons that define where the information held in the contact information comes from.

In other words, you now have a very powerful but simple to use contact management system.

When you add extra information to a contact it is only visible to you. Their profile won't be updated and all you are doing is making sure that the next time you chat online with them you have the most recent information about your online relationship easily to hand.

IMPORTED CONTACTS

One of the questions you may have is "what about all the business cards I've got stored away for people who aren't on LinkedIn yet?"

LinkedIn gives you the opportunity to import a contact list from any other system you use in the form of a CSV, TXT or VCF file. This means anyone you currently have stored in something like Outlook could be added to your LinkedIn account, even though they aren't on the LinkedIn network themselves.

To upload a contact database or list, first make sure it's in the correct format, then visit the *Add Contacts* section of your Connections Dashboard and select *Any Email*. At the end of the next page you will see a link to *Upload Contacts File*.

Timely Warning: Do bear in mind, if you add any sort of a contact database to your LinkedIn account, you might just broadcast the standard LinkedIn connection request to everyone on the list. My question to you is, why do it at all?

If you do decide to import a database, you can find the people you added by using the 'hidden' filter on your Network Dashboard. When and if, they get around to adding themselves to the network, using the email address you also have for them, then their headline and photograph will show up indicating that they have added a profile to the network. You can follow up with a connection request if you want to. Of course, by the time they get around to joining LinkedIn any reason for connecting may have long since evaporated and you may decide to delete them from your *hidden* filter instead.

In the meantime, all of the information you have about that person is stored on LinkedIn and you can easily send them an email by using the link next to their name in the *hidden* filter.

PROFILE ORGANISER

In this book, I have tried to avoid talking about any of the premium features a paid account provides on LinkedIn. The reason for this is the vast majority of features are available to the free user. However, there is one benefit which may make it worth having a professional subscription to LinkedIn and that is the Profile Organiser.

The *Profile Organiser* is what turns LinkedIn into a fully functional Contact Management System and it allows you to:-

- Add contacts to folders you create.

- Add prospects (people you aren't connected to at all) to folders.

In short, it allows you to keep a list of those people you are specifically working with or targeting in a handy list segmented to meet your needs.

You can watch what they are doing on LinkedIn to spot any opportunity to contact them; you can find references for them by searching the network and you can follow up on work you are already doing.

At the moment, I have folders for current clients, past clients, for local businesses and for my top prospects. I can create other folders, depending on changes to my business strategy, in the future.

For those without a professional subscription, it is worth knowing that correct use of the tagging system in your Contacts Dashboard to create filters for your contacts, gives you a fair degree of this functionality too, at no cost at all.

CHAPTER 7 - LINKEDIN GROUPS

Groups are one of the main powerhouses of LinkedIn. It is within groups you can begin the process of developing your voice and area of expertise. They also provide you with a place to network with others with the same interests, both personally and professionally. In fact, being part of a group will be one of the fastest ways to grow your network on LinkedIn as it automatically confers a degree of commonality with people you don't yet know.

When you log in to LinkedIn, you are presented with your home page, this lists the latest activity from people in your network; including their status updates, what they have commented on, who they have connected with, whether they have updated their profile, who has recommended whom and whether they have joined any groups. It allows you to see at a glance the groups' people deem worthwhile joining.

When you visit someone's profile you will also be able to see a list of groups they belong to, according to the visibility settings they have chosen for each group on their profile.

Groups fall into two broad areas:

- groups of your peers such as alumni or professional bodies

- groups around topics of interest

It would be fair to say you are unlikely to find a potential customer in a group containing your peers, but you may be able to use a group like this to establish yourself as an acknowledged expert within your industry. You may also be able to use such a group to develop collaborations.

Groups around interest will cover a broad spectrum of types, they may have a business or industry focus like engineering or accountancy, or they may be interested in a topic such as women's health.

I'd suggest you join one group from each category bearing in mind you don't have to remain a member of a group if you find it doesn't suit you.

To be effective in any group you must not be seen as just spamming the group by only adding links back to your own website, blog or content you've created. You need to add value to the group by taking part in discussions and sharing your own opinion to the mix already held. The advantage of this is you establish yourself very quickly as a relevant voice within this particular community.

You also need to think about starting interesting discussions, which are not necessarily focused on your own agenda but could demonstrate any underlying knowledge, experience, and expertise you may have around a related topic. An example of this might be requesting help to do some research into the needs of a particular customer group.

There are three ways to find a group (or several) to join. The first one is to click on the link that says Groups underneath the Interests link in menu two at the top of every page on LinkedIn. When you do this you'll be presented with a list of the groups you are currently a member of and on the right hand side you'll see a box containing brief details about groups you might be interested in. Clicking the 'more' link in this box takes you to a filtered search based on your current preferences, profile and groups.

The second is to use the *Groups You May Like* function you'll find presented on the right hand side of your LinkedIn home page. This works in a very similar way to the *People You May Know* function, selecting groups based on a combination of what you have written in your profile, and the groups you are already a member of.

You can also use the LinkedIn search facility in the top menu, using the drop-down menu on the left hand side to select the correct part of the LinkedIn network to search. Use keywords for your industry or company to find groups that may be appropriate. Remember, you may have to narrow your search down if you want to network only with people within your country or region.

The search results you get can be filtered through tick boxes on the left hand side of the screen. These filters allow you to find groups your connections are already members of, types of groups and languages used.

There are two types of groups. **Open groups**, as the name implies, are ones open to anyone within the LinkedIn community, and clicking *Join* will give you immediate and automatic access to the group. **Closed groups**, on the other hand, are indicated with a small padlock icon and clicking *Join* will send a request to the group administrator on your behalf. Some closed groups are for specific sets of professionals; it goes without saying, if you don't fit the criteria, have membership of the required body or institution, please don't bother requesting to join as you will be refused.

You'll be able to get a feel for each group as you browse the lists. Each listing shows you information such as how many people are in the group; whether any of your contacts are members; how many discussions are taking place and whether they are considered active.

When I'm looking for groups to join, the first thing I want to check is whether a group is active or not; there's nothing lonelier than long discussions with yourself.

Just because a group appears active, by the number of discussions, doesn't necessarily make it so. Every time someone adds a link back to a website, blog post or piece of news, a discussion is created; and there are some groups which are made up of nothing but such promotional activity. This is useful in moderation, but a good group is one where people actually talk to one another and engage in discussion about interesting and relevant topics. This is why it may take some time to find the right groups for you.

MY GROUPS

Once you have joined a group you can find it again by clicking on the Groups link from the Interests drop down menu at the top of every LinkedIn page. This takes you to your own Groups home page and will allow you to see at a glance the most recent activity on each.

You will notice underneath each group you have joined are a number of icons; the first is statistics for the group, the second is the number of discussions, the third is the number of jobs and the final set of icons are mini avatars of group members who have recently been active.

Clicking on the name of the group takes you to that specific group's home page and it is from here you can see every other part of the group. If you are a group manager, you will see an additional link allowing you to manage the group and change its settings.

You can also re-order the list of groups on your Groups home page to present the ones you like the most at the top of the page. To do so, click the link that says *Reorder* and then number the boxes on the left-hand side, bearing in mind number 1 will be at the top of the page.

GROUP ACTIVITY

When you visit one of your groups you have a number of different sections you can explore and the menu bar will display these for you.

Mostly, it should be fairly self-explanatory. For instance, *Discussions* will take you to the list of discussions taking place with the most recent and/or popular at the top of the list (you can switch between these two views by using the *Choose Your View* drop-down menu on the left-hand side of the page); selecting *Members* takes you to the list of members and *Search* allows you to search the archive of the group.

GROUP HOME PAGE

Clicking on the name of a group will take you to a specific group's home page. It is from here you will be able to monitor almost the entire activity taking place, including the discussions people are having. Getting involved in discussions is one of the fastest ways to ensure you are seen as an expert, or a good person to get involved or work with.

The most recent discussions (according to the view you choose) are displayed on the left-hand side of the home page. On the right-hand side you'll see the most recent activity of some people in the group.

You have the chance to get involved at the top of the home page every time you visit with the *Start Discussion / Poll* box. This is where you can begin a new discussion by adding a question, statement or observation; you can also add a link to an item of interest you think other members may find useful. The alternative is to create a *Poll* with five possible options as answers; polls are a great way to do some quick and dirty 'research' on a particular topic of interest to you.

Immediately underneath this update box is a section that scrolls through the most recent activity automatically, changing every three or four seconds.

On the right-hand side of the screen you will see there are updates from other members of the group. Further down you will also find a small notification box telling you who are the most influential people in the group at that moment in time. Influence, in this instance, is determined by such things as the number of times individuals get involved in discussions or add new items of interest.

DISCUSSIONS

When you click on the title of a discussion, you will be taken to another page which shows who asked the question, the question itself together with a little more information to expand it, and a series of comments from members that have already taken part. There will be a blank comment box at the bottom of the page and it's in here you write your own reply, which may be a suggestion, comment or an opinion. If necessary, you can also include links to external sites simply by typing in the whole web address for instance *http://www.lindaph.me*.

Sometimes, clicking on the discussion title may take you to a completely different website as this was a link to an external article, blog post or document. Occasionally, these can be helpful, often they aren't and it's what can make a potentially good group, really quite annoying.

If you want to be kept up to date with discussions, perhaps because you're interested in the topic under discussion, or if it's a subject that's particularly relevant, then you can tick the *'Send Me An Email for Each Comment'* box when you add your own reply. Alternatively, you can tick the *Follow* button which appears underneath the initial question.

If there is a discussion which you think is worthy of more attention, then you can share it with the wider group community by clicking on *Like*. When you do this your action appears in the update feed at the right-hand side of the page.

You can also use the *Flag* facility to highlight an inappropriate discussion, because it's a promotion, job or offensive for some other reason, to the group managers, who can then take action.

The purpose of a discussion is, naturally, to ask a question. This could be a leading question you already know the answer to; it could be a piece of research for which you might use the Poll option, or it could just be to start a debate. What is important though is the question entices people to respond to you.

When someone asks a particularly popular question it can get their name and photograph in front of an active and interested audience; this is the LinkedIn equivalent of presenting from the stage and is one of the reasons groups can be such a useful tool in growing a network of helpful individuals.

The more you participate, the more you ask interesting and helpful questions, the more you flag discussions you like and help people out, the faster your star will rise. More people will ask to connect with you, more people will follow your company and more people will get in touch with you.

Every time you start a discussion you can add links to other, relevant pieces of content such as articles or videos to illustrate the points you are making. You do this by selecting the *Attach a Link* option underneath the discussion box. This provides you with the facility to add a link to a piece of news, useful resource on an external website or other, public area of LinkedIn you think your fellow members might like. Once you have added the whole web address in the box, you simply click *Attach* and then *Share* and it will be made available on the home page of the group immediately. It will also be sent out in any group update emails sent to members according to their personal preferences.

Adding links like this can be a great way to build traffic to your website or blog, but only if they are appropriate to the general themes and discussions taking place. If they aren't, then you run the risk of the administrator removing the news item and/or banning you for spamming the members.

POLLS

Starting a Poll is a quick way to get some immediate feedback on a question or issue that has arisen; it's a great way to find simple statistics to inform a blog post, to gather opinion about something controversial for a news release or even to find out what the 'state of the nation' is when it comes to a particular topic.

You need to have five, reasonably easy to understand, choices to give your respondents; you can even make it time sensitive by setting an end date as well. Group members can then vote and comment at the same time, so you get the benefit of both quantitative and qualitative data. An example of a poll might be "How much business have you received as a result of working with the LinkedIn community?"

MEMBERS

Your group's *Members* page allows you to view all the members in your group, as well as who the current influencers are (these are people with the most to say or who participate the most). When you are a member of a group you will always appear at the top of the list, other members you're connected to directly will appear below you. Underneath them will be the list of members you aren't directly connected to (yet).

The list is one of the clearest ways to demonstrate the importance of having a great photo and 'headline', the strapline that appears at the top of your profile page; this is because it's these items which are most likely to entice people to view your profile, perhaps even asking you to connect.

PROMOTIONS

This is the section of a group devoted to members who want to promote something such as an event, product, service or a special offer. To use it select the *Post a Promotion* link on the right-hand side of the page.

Some groups are very well managed and will encourage members to use the various sections responsibly, taking promotions out of the general discussions list when necessary. Other groups aren't so well managed and it can be annoying to find a group where the discussions are just a constant stream of self promoting links back to services, products and offers.

I'd recommend not using such groups, you will get annoyed by the updates posted and will switch off to them; other members will do the same too meaning it's really not worth the effort.

JOBS

Not every group has a jobs board and it is at the discretion of the group administrators whether they include one or not. Often it will be dependent upon the purpose of the group and/or whether it is perceived to be a useful function. However, where they do exist they can be extremely useful for members allowing them to advertise their vacancies, as well as for those looking for employment to see what's on offer.

If you click on one of the job links, you should be taken to some further details explaining how to apply; this isn't always the case as it depends on the skill of the person posting the job advert.

You can post your own vacancy or request by using the *Post a Job Discussion* link in the top right of the page. This allows you to add a discussion to the group and is currently free of charge.

Using the *Post a Job* link instead will take you to a premium section of LinkedIn because posting jobs is a paid for facility on the network.

SEARCH

You can search the group discussions from this page. On the right-hand side you'll see a list of all the discussions in chronological order; on the left-hand side is a search box for keywords and a set of links filtering out specific types of content.

MORE

The More tab has a number of drop-down options including Updates, Your Activity, Your Settings, Sub Groups, Group Profile and Group Statistics. The most useful of these menu options is, in my opinion, *Updates* as this shows the most recent, chronologically ordered activity of all group members allowing you to spot those who are most active, quickly and easily. I can, if I choose, also enter the various discussions, engage and interact with my peers on the topics and subjects I am most interested in and thereby demonstrate my knowledge, experience, skill or general wit and wisdom.

YOUR ACTIVITY

This link takes you to a page which displays all of your activity in the group. If you have no recent activity you can use the links on the left-hand side to view things like *Discussions You've Started* to get a history, at least some, of your past activity. It can be quite sobering to realise you haven't been active for a year or two.

YOUR SETTINGS

This is where you can change all of the settings associated with your membership of a particular group, including how you wish to be kept updated about changes and activity. For instance, you may not wish to receive daily digests. You may also choose to turn off displaying the group on your profile, particularly if you are job hunting and don't want your employer to know.

SUBGROUPS

Subgroups are a subset of existing groups and they allow those that come in different flavours to sub divide by country, region or speciality. Most groups will never need to use this facility because they are contained by subject matter rather than by geographic location. Bear in mind if you do decide to join a sub-group you will automatically be given membership of (and access to) the parent group as well.

GROUP PROFILE

This is the page you may have visited when you first chose to join the group, especially if it were closed and had to ask permission to join. It gives an overview of the purpose of the group, a list of some members, the details of the group manager and a link to the *Group Statistics*.

GROUP STATISTICS

Statistics are always interesting, and can be very useful when you are active in the LinkedIn network. These statistics tell you things like the basic demographics of the group such as where most members are located, what their job type is and the industry they work in.

Knowing this data can mean the difference between spending your time in a group that's highly relevant to your needs, and a group made up of the wrong people. For instance, let's say you make widgets for the manufacturing sector, if all the members of the group work in the creative industries then the chances are you may not be as successful as you could be in a group where the members work in manufacturing. The same would be true of location, particularly if you are constrained by things like legal frameworks, which don't tend to travel beyond geographic boundaries.

It's now time to find relevant groups for you to join; before you do you must think about why you are joining them. Revisit your overall objective for using LinkedIn, the one you identified in Chapter 1 of this book. Finding groups that will help you meet your objective is critical, because you will be far more likely to engage with them on a regular basis, if you do.

Use LinkedIn search to find groups which can best meet your needs by using keywords from your industry to identify them. An alternate way to find relevant groups is to study the profiles of your network members to see which groups they are members of.

Don't forget groups can be based all over the world and may not have other professionals in your country as a member. You need to take a view on whether this is relevant or not. For instance, you could be the only professional based in your country in the group and therefore gain an international reputation; or you might want to work within a specific legal framework that isn't appropriate or functional, outside the country you work or live in.

It might be helpful to pick a few key areas you think will help you meet the objective you identified. For instance, the things I'd like to focus on might include women's health, social media, small and medium sized businesses, social enterprise and publishing.

These are the keywords and phrases I could use in the LinkedIn search facility to find relevant groups.

One of my objectives is to grow the membership of The Hysterectomy Association; the fact I already know my target audience, women having surgery, are unlikely to want their co-contacts to know they have medical problems, means I would have little success in encouraging them to use a group created for them. However, my aim is to educate women about the choices they have, and at the same time ensure they find the association before they have the operation.

As one thing that must happen before a hysterectomy can be scheduled in the UK is referral to a surgeon by a GP, I could, therefore, find LinkedIn groups with a special interest in Women's Health who might help me get my message to GP's and Surgeons.

Which is the audience best placed help you meet your objectives? Try to join only one or two; otherwise you won't have the time to really get to know them. A good tip is to use keywords, within the search bar at the top of every page, specific to your industry; for example, I might use medicine, medical, gynaecology, general practitioner etc. Remember you can use the drop-down menu next to the search bar to select, People, Jobs, Companies, Inbox (your own inbox), Groups and Updates.

SHOULD I START A GROUP?

Many people quite like the idea of starting their own group on LinkedIn; they feel (quite rightly) it is a great way to gain exposure not only for themselves, but also for their skills and abilities, as well as their interests and business.

However, I would say this needs to be treated with caution. Anyone can start a group, it is easy to do so, but it takes time, effort and organisation to maintain it, grow it and keep it vibrant.

I manage groups on LinkedIn on behalf of clients and I need to access the groups every day to monitor membership requests, moderate the discussions, start and encourage discussions, invite new members and generally nurture them into self-sustaining growth. It takes around twelve months of hard and daily work, to get a group to a level where it no longer needs a nursemaid.

If you don't have the time to devote to this activity, please reconsider starting a group and consider joining an existing one instead, it will be a far more enjoyable and profitable experience.

CHAPTER 8 - PROMOTING YOUR LINKEDIN PROFILE

Promoting your LinkedIn profile can be as simple as creating a LinkedIn button for your website or blog and adding the web address for your profile to your email signature.

Alternatively, you can make it a whole lot more complex by doing such things as:

- Adding your LinkedIn profile address (or button) to any other profiles on social networks/social media you are a member of.

- Adding it to your signature on any forums or other discussion groups you happen to belong to, particularly if they have a professional element to them.

- Making sure your profile settings are set to show your *Full Profile*, as this is indexed by the search engines.

- Inviting more people to join you; as you do so, they'll get to know about your LinkedIn activity too.

- Becoming active on groups.

- Adding your public profile URL to your email signature, curriculum vitae, resume, portfolio, promotional literature, business card and stationary.

- Adding your public profile URL to any presentations and proposals you put together – particularly if you have relevant recommendations and/or experience listed on your profile.

Don't forget to create your personalised profile URL; you can revisit how to do this in Chapter 3, Getting Started.

CREATING A LINKEDIN BUTTON FOR YOUR BLOG OR WEBSITE

You can also create a handy little graphical icon for your blog or website that links directly to your public profile page.

1. Click the Profile link in the top navigation bar of the website.

2. Click *Manage Public Profile Settings* from the *Edit* drop-down menu next to *Improve Your Profile*.

3. Scroll down the page and select *Profile Badges*, you can find this underneath your *Public Profile URL* on the right-hand side of the screen.

This shows you a variety of buttons and the code next to them, when you have chosen the one you want simply click once in the box with the code next to the image you want, then press *CTRL* and *C* on your keyboard; this will copy the code for you.

4. Next, login to the dashboard of your blog or website and add it to the page, sidebar or text widget, 'pasting' it in its entirety according to whichever element your particular system happens to use.

Alternatively, send the code you copied by email to your website developer and ask them to add it to the appropriate page for you.

5. Click *Save* and then *Close*.

CHAPTER 9 - ADVANCED LINKEDIN PROFILES

If LinkedIn is the place to showcase your professional career, business, skills and expertise, it would make sense for it to provide multiple ways to showcase the different aspects for your working life.

They could have chosen the route of creating a number of systems allowing you to write articles, show presentations and have meetings within the application. In fact they did this up until the end of 2012. Nowadays though, they have chosen to include some essential elements, such as adding in the details of publications, courses and voluntary work and also allow you to create links to other documents and portfolio items within your profile itself. This is a great example of only doing what you are good at, and not trying to be all things to all men.

Welcome to the world of Rich Media, Profile Sections, Recommendations and Endorsements, Status Updates and RSS Feeds.

So, what sort of activities do these functions allow you to do? Briefly, they allow you to share presentations and videos you have created on your profile, they allow you to highlight achievements you are proud of, they give others the chance to tell the world how great you are and they help you begin promoting yourself and your cause across the network. It's a great way to share knowledge and expertise.

You can also add articles and blog posts you have written to your activity updates, this allows members of your network to read your articles, and learn more about you and your business.

RICH MEDIA

You can now add a wide variety of what LinkedIn calls Rich Media content to your profile in the *Summary*, *Education* and *Experience* sections. To use this feature, your content must be loaded on another external service, this could be your own website or it could be in a network such as Slideshare or YouTube. The types of media you can add include documents, images, presentations (PowerPoint style) and videos.

Every time you add one of these documents to your profile it is added to what's called your *Professional Gallery*. This is a pop-up section of your profile and it shows the current selection in the main window, with a sliding gallery of other media you've added below it. Viewers can then scroll through selecting items of interest as they go. Although you may add a presentation you created for one role against a particular job you've had, it is still available to view whenever anyone loads your *Professional Gallery* by clicking on a media item somewhere else in your profile.

You might be wondering why you would want to add Rich Media items to your profile; in a word it's about expertise. Nothing says 'expert' or 'professional' like a well crafted presentation, a perfectly written document or demonstrates understanding like an explanatory video.

The only thing you need to bear in mind before getting started is whether you have the right to load the content. Just because you created a presentation when you worked at XYZ Company, does not mean you have the copyright to show it on your profile. You will therefore need to check with your employer first.

If you already have a bunch of presentations or videos you would like to share then the best thing to do is get started. You can add Rich Media by visiting your Profile page in *Edit* mode, scrolling to the section (Summary, Experience or Education) you would like to add your media to and then clicking the *Square + Box Icon* you can find next to the title, or section, you are updating. Add the full web address or locate the file on your computer for the content you have created and press the return key, your media is now added to that section, as well as to your *Professional Gallery*.

PROFILE SECTIONS

When you view your profile in edit mode, you won't fail to notice the additional sections you can add to your profile; these are listed on the right-hand side of the screen when you are in *Edit Profile* mode. Some of these have taken over from popular applications; mostly however, they are new. The sections you can add include: Projects, Languages, Test Scores, Courses, Patents, Certifications, Publications, Honors and Awards, Skills and Expertise, Volunteer Experience and Causes, and finally, Organisations.

Each section is designed to fill out a little more information about what makes you an individual unique in the world; they should be used primarily for profile/business related information and materials only.

Projects - The definition of 'project' is something with a beginning and end date delivering something specific. Therefore taking on a new role at work is not a project however, developing and delivering a new piece of software is. Projects could be something you have done within a period of employment, something you are working on from home or even a part of a student portfolio. If you are going to use this section please do fill out all the details, including the description. It might also be interesting for readers to find out more about any challenges you faced and obstacles you overcame.

Languages - This is the place to list second languages you speak fluently. There is no point in adding English, if English is your mother tongue, unless of course the need to be able to communicate clearly is an important part of your overall profile. Therefore I wouldn't add English to my portfolio, but an English teacher (who happens to be British) might.

Test Scores - In some professions and academic institutions, test scores are an intrinsic part of the process you go through towards qualification. If your SAT scores are important for your career path, then I'd recommend listing them.

Courses - For some careers you are expected to have undertaken some professional development courses, these are usually formal qualifications or events that show you understand the fundamentals of the profession to the qualification level gained. In other instances, you may have undertaken specific training to help develop your career. All courses you have taken, for which you have received recognition through an accredited process (other than formal education) should be listed, if they are relevant to who you are, what you do or where you plan to go in the future.

Patents - A Patent is an acknowledgement by an official body that a particular person can be credited with inventing a particular thing, process or system. It is essential, particularly in the manufacturing industry, if you are planning to sell something new to the market. If you hold a patent or you have an application pending then you can list it in this section, this may open doors to offers you might not otherwise have access to.

Certification - Some industries require you to be certified as competent to practice. Typically, these will be renewable on a regular basis. If you have such a requirement then you can add this to your profile as potential employers will be able to search across the LinkedIn network.

Publications - Have you been published, either as a contributor to a book or journal or as an author in your own right? If so, then you can list your publications in this section. You can also add links to the relevant publications, if they can be found online, making it easy for anyone to follow up on your contributions.

Honors and Awards - This could mean different things to different people; in the UK it might be an award of MBE (Member of the British Empire) bestowed by the reigning monarch; in the US it might be related to your College Alumni status. Generally, these are public acknowledgements made to 'worthy' individuals.

Volunteer Experience and Causes - Employers and other third sector organisations value the ability to see what experience you might have had in the things you are passionate about. There are two sections, the first relates to any experience you might have, such as volunteering on your child's school committee or in a local charity shop. The second section allows you to list organisations you are passionate about and support on a regular basis.

Organisations - This is the section of your profile that allows you to list any other organisations you are a member of, where they are relevant to your business persona. These might include professional bodies, Membership organisations, Chambers of Commerce or even Business Networks.

It goes without saying, I hope, that these sections should only be added where they have a direct relevance to who you are on LinkedIn. Your profile informs other people about who you are, what you do and why you do it; therefore the ideal content to add to these sections is information which supports this persona.

Now, you may be someone just starting out on your working journey and may be wondering about the sorts of things you can fill out your profile with. Often people fear they don't have enough to say about themselves because they perceive a lack of obvious experience. Well, it's time to think outside the box.

We all gather experience in many different ways, for instance the housewife or husband often has experience of time management, budgeting and conflict resolution; what matters in our working life is how these experiences are applied in different instances. For example, could someone with experience in conflict resolution apply their skills to the world of negotiation? Could someone with experience in budgeting apply their skills in the world of project management?

Taking a sideways look at the abilities you have developed and the knowledge you have gained like this may help you to spot opportunities you hadn't realised existed before.

RECOMMENDATIONS

LinkedIn Recommendations are a way of acknowledging the contribution people within your network have made to some aspect of your life. This could be personal, or it could be business based.

A recommendation is rather like a testimonial; it is written and displayed on your profile against a specific role. It is also displayed in the overall list of recommendations in chronological order. You can request a recommendation from people you have worked with, or they can 'pay it forward' by writing you a recommendation without your having to ask for it. You can also write a recommendation for someone whose service you have valued.

However, it pays to have some guidelines for what you will and will not do; this is because it's common to be sent requests for such recommendations by people who have never worked with you, or those who have not provided a good service.

I would also advise you don't fall into the trap of providing reciprocal recommendations, that is you provide a recommendation for someone and they (almost immediately) write one for you; these appear one after the other on your network members home pages and it's easy to spot where there has been some recommendation spamming taking place.

To request a recommendation:

1. Login to LinkedIn.

2. Go to *Recommendations* which you will find under the Profile link in the top navigation bar.

3. Click on *Request Recommendation*.

4. Choose a member of your network to ask.

5. Personalise the request, giving them enough information about why you would like their support.

6. Click *Send*.

Once you have sent your recommendation request you can sit back and wait with bated breath for the response. When it arrives, you'll be sent an email informing you you've received a recommendation; it is up to you to decide whether you want to display it on your profile or not.

To give a recommendation in advance of being asked for it

1. Login to LinkedIn.

2. Go to *Recommendations* and click on *Sent Recommendations*.

3. Scroll to the bottom of the page and complete the wizard you find there.

4. Click *Send*.

LinkedIn Endorsements

LinkedIn Endorsements are rather like the ubiquitous Facebook 'Like' button, and are a different way of acknowledging the skills you know people in your network have.

When you were completing your profile you will have added a number keywords and phrases in the skills and expertise section. A selection of these keywords is presented to your network whenever they visit the profiles of people they are connected to at a first level. All they need to do is select the skills they believe you have, click the *Endorse* button and their profile picture automagically appears on your profile page, next to the skill they have confirmed they believe you have. As more people endorse you for a particular skill, the number increases on the left-hand side.

You can do the same for your network. The next time you visit someone's profile, if the endorse box pops up and you know from experience the person has the skills you are being shown, simply click 'endorse' and your face will show on their profile for other people to see.

It goes without saying, those whose profiles are viewed more frequently by others, will be the people who get the opportunity to be 'endorsed' more frequently.

You can also endorse people for skills they haven't listed, simply by using the box provided to do so. Recently, I was endorsed by a member of my network for the skill 'Friendly Demeanour'. Although I regularly communicate with them on LinkedIn, Twitter and in Skype conversations we have never actually met; I believe this says a lot about what this particular person values about me.

This mechanism is a great way to get visibility in other parts of the network you may not have access too; however use it wisely, as you need to be certain the people you are endorsing do indeed have the skills you say they do. Remember, recommending something to someone which then turns out to be the wrong thing will backfire on you, as people begin to distrust the things you say.

Every time you spend a little time endorsing someone, or they endorse you, a notification appears on your reciprocal networks home pages, allowing people you may not even know yet, to see their connection values you.

Endorsements are, I believe, the logical extension of a profile listing the skills people have. But what exactly are skills (as understood by LinkedIn)? And how do Endorsements compare with Recommendations?

I think I would define a skill in this sense as something used in the course of a job or business on behalf of clients or customers. It might also be an area of acknowledged expertise, experience and knowledge rather than something one happens to do or know.

What's the difference between Endorsements and Recommendations?

Simply put, an *Endorsement* is given for skills **I** say I have and a *Recommendation* is a compliment given by someone else telling the world more about how **they** value me and our working relationship. The difference is in who's making the initial statement, and I believe this informs the value with which we might understand their context.

Giving an endorsement is quick and simple; you just click the button to say you agree they have the skill indicated. Giving a recommendation on the other hand requires the person to write something more definitive; this is harder and demonstrates more of a commitment to the recipient.

The difficulty with both of these features is one of reciprocity, too often even these days' I see person B recommending person A simply because they've received a recommendation from them. The same is happening with endorsements. It's very easy to get 'click happy', as often when you view the profiles of your network members, LinkedIn asks you to 'endorse people'. In fact, when I decided to see what was happening, I was surprised at the number of my connections who all listed 'social media' as a skill; in the majority of cases it's not a skill I've seen in evidence amongst those claiming it.

LINKEDIN TODAY AND INFLUENCERS

When you are on your home page in LinkedIn, you will see a section at the top which is split into three areas showing LinkedIn Today news recommended for you on the left-hand side, and two Influencer posts.

LinkedIn Today is a news feed from a specific list of sources of news updates and blog posts it thinks are relevant to you. This is tailored to the sort of things the network as a whole share and like, and the industry you have selected for your profile. You can also personalise it with updates from specific people or topics.

You can find your personal LinkedIn Today home page at *linkedin.com/today/*. This page is personalised with news from the industries you have chosen to follow. You can change some of the news you see on LinkedIn Today by visiting *linkedin.com/today*. Simply follow or unfollow individual people you find on the *All Influencers* page.

You can also choose to follow news by channel, simply visit the *All Channels* page and tick those you are most interested in.

You can also choose to remove some types of updates from your home page altogether by editing the relevant sections of the Settings Dashboard; these are found in the *Customize the Updates You See on your Home page* section of the *Accounts* settings. If you prefer, you can also follow individual news sources such as the BBC or Brisbane Times.

Influencers on LinkedIn are invited to contribute unique articles on LinkedIn Today, these articles are contained within the LinkedIn website and don't appear elsewhere on the Web. These people are considered by LinkedIn to be thought leaders, influencing large numbers of people across a diverse range of market sectors.

CHAPTER 10 - CRAFTING EFFECTIVE UPDATES

Status Updates are the most common of all social networking activities; you will have the ability to tell your connections, fans, and followers what you are doing on every single network, and LinkedIn is no exception. Regardless of the network, they are designed to allow contacts to keep up to date with what's happening amongst other people they share some sort of online relationship with. In LinkedIn, they will primarily be based around business interest, showing latest posts, whose connected to whom, who has been endorsed or joined a group. It allows you to find out more about what people are planning to do and what they are interested in whenever they update their profile.

If you see something you think is interesting you can add a comment, you can contact the author, you can share the update more widely (on your profile and to Twitter in some cases, in a group you're a member of or to a sub-section of your contacts, if it's relevant) or you can 'like' it. In this instance, clicking the *Like* button is the same as flagging it to your network and saying 'this is worth reading'.

Whenever you add a status update, comment on another, like or share something, this action becomes a part of the *Activity Stream* you can find on your Profile page. The person whose comment you've acted on receives a notification you have done something through the notifications 'flag' you'll be able to see at the top of every page of your LinkedIn account.

If you comment on something, this message is also made visible to the author, his network and yours as well. If you share something it can appear as either a status update on your profile, in a group if you choose to share it there, or as an email to the contacts you choose to send it on to.

At the moment, my observation is that status updates are rarely used effectively, but they are a fantastic way to start building stronger relationship with people in your network. They are also a great way to keep your name in front of your connections on a regular basis.

You can add a status update to LinkedIn from the top of your home page. When you add an update it will appear in the stream of activity on your connections home pages as well, rather like those appearing on your own home page, until it is superseded by others coming along later in the day. They may also be added to the weekly LinkedIn Network Updates email you, and your network, receive. It is also worth knowing that you have some limited functionality when it comes to who sees your update; the drop down box underneath the update box will allow you to have a message added to LinkedIn, LinkedIn + Twitter (if Twitter is enabled) or just your Connections.

WHAT MAKES A STATUS UPDATE EFFECTIVE?

It's a difficult question and the effects will be highly dependent on how good, or strong, your network is; for instance if no-one in your network is particularly active then the chances of them responding or sharing are slim. However, if you use keywords in your update you could interest someone, who knows someone who might be interested.

An effective status update is one which encourages another person to do something such as sharing, liking, commenting or sending you a message.

Bear in mind if you want your status update to go out to Twitter as well, then it will need to be kept under 140 characters, including any links you have added.

TEN SUGGESTIONS FOR STATUS UPDATES ON LINKEDIN

1. Insert the title and a link to one of your recent blog articles.

2. Insert the title and a link to an article or website you read and really like.

3. Share a great "quote of the day."

4. Give a brief piece of advice relevant to your brand, or area of speciality.

5. Share a link to an educational YouTube video or slideshare presentation. Do make sure the ones you choose are a. relevant to your profile and b. shorter than a couple of minutes as attention spans are dropping.

6. Use a status update as a way of sharing important announcements about you or your company in a headline format. This is particularly useful if you are writing a press release and want to get it out to a broader audience.

7. Add links to articles in which you were quoted, or in which you participated. This could also be a link to a guest post you have written for another website

8. Use them to share some worthy and exciting news at work or in your business, such as "Just landed a great new social media professional development client this week and looking forward to the challenge"

9. You could also use status updates to support a cause you are passionate about as well

10. Finally, are you looking for a job, do you have a vacancy to fill; do you need a new supplier or recommendation? All of these could be sensible and effective uses of your status update box.

Don't forget to ensure content you share from others, whether it's a blog post, news article or video, is consistent with what you say you're interested in on your profile. Random updates about unrelated subject areas will have little effect in the long term.

Once a status update has been created it will be visible on other people's LinkedIn home pages for a short period of time, before it is superseded by the next update made. They will remain on your profile's *Activity Stream* for up to fifteen days, depending on how many you post, and are only visible to those who are logged in to LinkedIn; they never appear on your public profile and can't be indexed by the search engines.

You can also control which levels of connection see individual updates by using the *Visible To* dropdown menu near the share box. It is worth noting you may have to start typing to see this menu. Finally, you can set overall visibility of your updates from the *Profile* section of the Settings Dashboard.

If visibility is set to "everyone", your update may appear:

- on the home pages of your 1st-degree connections

- on the home pages of your 2nd or 3rd degree connections if re-shared, commented upon, or liked

- in the activity feed on your profile page

- on LinkedIn Today

If visibility is set to "Your connections", your update may appear:

- on the home pages of your 1st degree connections

- in the activity feed on your profile page.

CONNECTING EXTERNAL ACCOUNTS TO UPDATES

There are a few external services you can connect directly to your LinkedIn account, these allow you to post status updates automatically whenever you add content to the third-party service.

WORDPRESS

For those who aren't familiar with it, WordPress is my favourite blogging tool. It gives millions the opportunity to present their thoughts and opinions on almost any topic to the world, in a very simple and easy to use system. If you fancy having a go at blogging, just head on over to those nice people at www.wordpress.com and grab an account.

To automatically add your WordPress blog to your status updates, you will need to use the Publicize feature of WordPress.com or the Jet Pack Plugin, a third-party account such as TwitterFeed or Dlvr.it if you host your own WordPress website. You can find Publicize by logging into WordPress and going to Share setting of WordPress Settings.

TRIPIT

Tripit is a travel companion application that helps you to plan business trips. It will automatically send a status update out on LinkedIn when you embark on your next trip, thus affording your network connections the chance to see it and perhaps say 'fancy meeting for a coffee?'

To add Tripit status updates on LinkedIn, you will need to visit *tripit.com/uhp/linkedInMyTravel* and connect the two accounts. Every time you add a new trip to Tripit, it will be posted as a LinkedIn status update.

SLIDESHARE

Slideshare is a social network that allows you to share presentations and documents. It's a little like YouTube without the video. You can link your Slideshare account to LinkedIn in two ways. The first is to connect the accounts so whenever you add a new presentation or document it automatically sends a status update out on LinkedIn.

The second way is manually driven, allowing you to add your presentations and documents as Rich Media elements on your profile. Just use the link provided for each item you want to add and they will be added to the *Professional Portfolio* on your profile.

A WORD ABOUT RSS FEEDS

You can find the RSS feeds (a special web address which lists all the most recent content) all over LinkedIn. These feeds allow you to keep up to date with your networks status updates in a feed reader. However, LinkedIn has been removing RSS capability from the network over the last twelve months and it may be these options disappear in the not too, distant future.

CHAPTER 11 - SEARCHING LINKEDIN

You can search LinkedIn for a wide variety of content and profile. For instance you can search for people, groups, jobs and companies.

Searching for specific individuals, groups and companies is generally done from the search box in the top menu bar. You will notice on the left-hand side of the search box there is a drop-down menu, the default word is 'People', but you can also select things like Companies, Groups, Inbox, etc...

You can add anything to the search box and, if you don't know the name of the person, the specific company or group, you can use keywords.

LinkedIn will try to be helpful and, as you type, it will come up with suggestions for you based on the words you are typing; rather like using predictive text on a mobile phone. Unless they show the specific thing you are looking for, the best solution is to type to the end of your word or phrase and click on the magnifying glass, as this will bring up the entire list of results for your search. You can turn off LinkedIn Search's predictive capabilities by using the drop-down menu item on the search box that says *Turn off Suggestions*.

When you are given a list of search results you will find the left-hand side of the page contains a number of different filters you can apply to the results. These include language, location, company or industry, depending on the search you are performing.

Make sure you tick (or untick) the relevant sections to narrow your search down.

If you want to be very specific, say searching for agricultural professionals within a 50 mile radius of Aberdeen in the UK, you would use the *Advanced Search* facility which you can find by clicking the link 'Advanced Search' next to the search box.

You can also enter a keyword in the search box at the top of the left-hand filters. So, if you are searching for groups in the UK you will almost certainly need to add the word 'UK' to your main keyword in this box to narrow the results down even further.

NOTE: if you are searching for people you already have in your existing network, you can narrow the results for your keyword down by de-selecting the connection levels at the top of the *People Search Results Page*. You can deselect first, second and third level connections, this then filters them out of your results list, hopefully making it much easier to spot the person you were looking for.

CHAPTER 12 - LINKEDIN COMPANY PAGES

LinkedIn is primarily a network for people, if you imagine yourself walking into a business network meeting, then LinkedIn is the virtual equivalent of this. In the most recent round of updates, the Company Profile became a Company Page and, as a result, a more coherent and larger part of the LinkedIn network.

Following one of the links to a Company from a personal profile will take you to the home page for that company; this gives you an overview of the company, its employees, products and insights. You may also find a representative of the company, usually the person who manages the page, has added Company Status Updates to an activity stream.

The company insights, you as a visitor to their page will be able to see, include who has changed jobs, a list of former employees you might know (useful for job hunters) and other company pages visitors viewed. Insights for a company page administrator give a much more detailed view.

If your company or business doesn't yet have a profile listed, it is easy to add one by clicking on the *Add Company* link you will find on the Companies home page at *linkedin.com/companies*.

This takes you to a simple form containing standard information such as the year the company was founded, number of employees, an overview and contact details. However, if you are an employee of a large company then you might not be the right person to create this profile and you will need to talk to the marketing, or HR departments to see if there is someone more appropriate to undertake the task.

Whenever a member, or ex-member, of your company signs up for LinkedIn and adds your company name to their list of past, or current, positions they will be invited to select from the names of similar companies that have already signed up. When they select one of these companies it will be added to the experience section of their profile as a clickable link, this takes a visitor to that company page on LinkedIn.

It is worth ensuring that all your employees know what the right name for the company is otherwise you will find you have people missing.

One of the benefits of LinkedIn Company pages is being able to use this as a resource to identify the correct person to contact; you can quickly see who is a member of your own network and what level removed they are from you. Once you identify someone it becomes much easier to ask them who you should speak to about your request, or to ask for an introduction to the correct member of staff.

COMPANY STATUS UPDATES

Having a company page allows you to publish company wide status updates, which are sent to your company follower's home page. You can use this as an opportunity to keep staff and followers (those who have chosen to 'follow' your company by clicking the *Follow* button) updated about your latest offers, news about new employees, useful information or changes being made. Only company page administrators can add a status update and, if you don't see a blank status update box at the top of the company page you don't have the authority to add an update.

Unlike personal status updates, you have much more capacity to target a company status update to go to everyone, or just a selected demographic. This allows you to send an update just to followers who are employed by large or small companies, who are in one of 100 possible industry sectors, who are in a particular function in their company (for instance research), who are at a particular level or who are in a specific geographic area. To set a targeted company status update simply select targeted from the *Share This* drop-down menu under the status update box.

LinkedIn also allow company status updates to include documents and images directly uploaded to the LinkedIn servers. However, it might be worth considering what happens when you do add something to LinkedIn in this way; who now owns the document or image, once it has been uploaded?

The reason I ask the question is because Facebook, another social network, has come under scrutiny for its use of members' data and the images they have shared with family and friends. Perhaps, it might be wise to share only those images and documents which are already in the public domain.

If you do decide to upload images and documents through a company status update, when visitors click on them, they will open in a pop-up window showing the uploaded media together with any comments that have been made and the numbers of people who have liked or shared this particular update.

Every status update added to a company profile comes with a mini set of statistics below it. These are only visible to the page administrator and include the number of impressions (times it was seen by someone), the number of clicks on a link, the number of interactions (liking, commenting or pinning) and the amount of engagement as a percentage.

TOP TEN TIPS FOR EFFECTIVE COMPANY STATUS UPDATES

1. Send updates out regularly, this increases engagement and interaction.

2. Status updates which are brief and that have a link and call to action lead to greater levels of engagement.

3. Use a variety of different content types, for instance newsletters, press releases, blog posts, news about staff. You can also share industry news and observations.

4. Ask your employees what they think should be included; give them a voice by asking them to contribute articles which can be shared.

5. Use status updates to raise awareness of other uses of LinkedIn, such as groups you manage, jobs you are recruiting for, products and services you are highlighting and staff you are recommending.

6. If people respond to your updates make sure you reply to those comments, it encourages further engagement. Remember everyone is seeking attention and validation in the social networking world.

7. Use the Insights section of your company page to identify the content driving the most engagement. What do people like? What gets most comments? Change your updates to reflect these subjects.

8. Use the Analytics section of the company page to identify the posts that created the most engagement and write more about them.

9. Ask your employees to share updates by liking them, commenting on them and posting them to their personal status updates and Twitter account. This helps to spread the word.

10. Just because your favourite time for posting to LinkedIn happens to be in the evening, doesn't mean it's the right time for the people you're trying to reach. Try to match business hours, around lunchtime and before the end of the day. Avoid Monday mornings and Friday afternoons because these are the times traditionally associated with catching up and preparation, there will not necessarily be as much engagement on the networks because of this.

PRODUCTS AND SERVICES

Administrators can add the details of products and services to a company page. These are full of information such as images, descriptions, links to more information, links to buy (if it's a product), lists of key features, promotional videos from YouTube and even special offers or promotions for individual items.

Once a product or service has been added, they can gather their own recommendations. You will see a *Recommend* button next to each item; if you are the administrator you will be encouraged to *Request Recommendations*.

INSIGHTS

When you are a page administrator, you will also have access to a two sets of statistics which gives you information about who is following you, how often your page is visited, former employees and how well individual status updates are performing.

To view this data:

- Go to your company page.

- Click the down arrow next to the *Edit* button in the upper right.

- Select *View follower insights* or *View page insights*.

The Follower Data shows:

Total Followers: This is the total number of people following your company page. As the number is only updated every 24 hours, it may be different from the number on the Overview tab.

New Followers Last 7 Days: This shows the number of people who started following your company page in the last seven days.

Updates Last 7 Days: This shows the number of status updates added to your company page over the previous seven days.

Total Impressions Last 7 Days: This number gives you the total number of times people have liked, clicked, commented on, or shared one of your company status updates. It is divided by the number of impressions for that update.

Impressions/Update Last 7 Days: This is the average number of impressions per company update over the last seven days.

Update Engagement Last 7 Days: The engagement rate is a calculation of the number of likes, clicks, comments and shares on your company updates, divided by the impressions in the last seven days.

Members Following: This shows the cumulative growth of the follower base over a twelve month period.

New Followers: The number of followers who have been added on a monthly basis.

Company Update Engagement: The total number of clicks, likes, comments, shares, and engagement rates over time. It shows six months worth of data and you can scroll back to see the previous six months

Company Update Impressions: The total number of company updates impressions over the previous twelve months. It shows six months worth of data and you can scroll back to see the previous six months

Follower Demographics: This is a breakdown of your company page followers by Seniority, Industry, Function, Region, Company Size, and Employee. Choose the tab at the top of the box to switch between each section.

Recent Followers: These are the profiles of your company page three most recent followers. You can click on *See More* to get a complete list of followers.

Each of these updates is affected by the increase or decrease from the previous seven days. Where there is no data to view, you will see a big banner across the section telling you so.

The Page Insights data shows:

Page Views Last 7 Days: This figure represents the number of times your company page has been viewed in the last seven days.

Unique Visitors Last 7 Days: This is the number of unique visitors to your company page in the last seven days, plus the increase or decrease from the previous 7 days.

Page Clicks Last 7 Days: This figure represents the number of times your company page has been clicked in the last seven days.

Page Views: This is the total number of page views for the different sections of your company page over twelve months. You can split out the data by the careers and products/services sections.

Unique Visitors: This area shows the total number of unique visitors to your company page over twelve months. You can split out the data by the careers and products/services sections.

Career Page Clicks: This data shows the number of times visitors to the page have clicked on jobs you have added, specific employees, any promotional banners links, or specific recruiters added to the career page.

Page Visitor Demographics: This section gives administrators an opportunity to see a more detailed summary of specific demographics of the people who visit your company page. Data is collated by seniority, industry, function, region, company size, and employee over twelve months.

Product & Services Page Clicks: This shows the total number times the *Get More Info* link, *Contact Us* link and any other promotions links added to your products & services section were clicked, over a twelve month period.

You can find the page Analytics by clicking on the link in the menu for your company page. The information you'll find here includes the same mini statistics you can find underneath each update on the company LinkedIn home page plus information about the number of followers acquired as a result of reading the update.

Company pages tend not to be helpful for most small businesses; this is probably because such businesses tend to promote the individuals within the team far more than the business itself. They may also perceive they have little time to add an extra set of updates to a small set of followers and employees.

For the larger company with several dozen members of staff, company pages can be very useful indeed, particularly because they have a larger group of people with which to share the burden of promotion.

CHAPTER 13 – LINKEDIN RECIPES FOR SUCCESS

In the coming pages I want to share some specific 'recipes' you can follow. These will help you be more effective at a wide range of activities that can help you in your business or your career (and sometimes both).

The list below shows how the recipes have been organised. To use them, choose the topics of most interest to you and then choose one of the strategies listed to work with first. You may want (or need) to do more than one to achieve the objectives and goals you have in mind, but it is important to focus on just one to start with.

Building a Business

- Create a Successful Collaboration.

- Market Your Business.

- Market Your Website.

Networking for Success

- Become an Industry Expert.

- Build Brand 'You'.

- Create an Engaging Headline.

Research and Development

- New Products and Services.

- Find People.

- Continuing Professional Development.

Job Hunting

- Find a Job.

- Create a Brilliant Portfolio.

- Find a Potential Employer.

You can find more updates about using LinkedIn effectively and other 'recipes for successes' at *womanontheedgeofreality.com*, which is my personal blog.

BUILDING A BUSINESS

There are many different actions and activities required to build a business. This set of recipes will concentrate on:

- Creating a Successful Collaboration.

- Marketing your Business.

- Marketing your Website.

Each of these activities is designed to ensure you, and your business, are in front of the right people at the right time.

CREATE A SUCCESSFUL COLLABORATION

According to dictionaries, to collaborate, in this sense, means to work jointly with others, or to cooperate with an agency or organisation with which you are not directly connected. In other words, this is a working partnership to achieve a single goal or aim. It might be the delivery of a particular product or service to a specific client. An example of successful collaborations might be the author who works with an illustrator; or the website developer who works with a graphic designer, photographer and a copywriter. None of these are permanent business relationships; they are simply formed to deliver a specific outcome.

The activities one would need to undertake to create a successful collaboration are:

- Find people with whom one shares similar values and ethics.

- Ensure those people have the skills needed to complete the work.

- Check the quality of work undertaken and their ability to deliver on time and to budget.

Therefore the actions one needs to take are:

1. Create a project brief that is as specific as you are able to make it. This should include requirements, skills set, time scales, location and any other pertinent information. You could upload this as a company status update or as a piece of Rich Media on your profile if it isn't confidential.

2. Undertake a search for individuals or companies within your network who have the required skill set. This may mean searching by keyword for specific terminology.

3. Post a status update asking your network for suggestions about suitable suppliers, you can also send individuals a direct request, or ask a question in a relevant group or LinkedIn Answers.

4. When you have a list of possible candidates, read their profiles and check any links they may have provided to their business websites, portfolios or other online materials.

5. Identify the skills, knowledge and understanding they claim to have and then check this against other industry specialists.

6. Read any recommendations and check their activity in any groups you have access to

7. View any endorsements they have, check the profiles of the people giving them to see if you feel they are genuine.

8. Create a shortlist of possible candidates and then contact them individually to find out if they are interested in the type of work of you are proposing and are able to deliver within the time frame you specify.

9. Ask possible candidates to send you a formal written proposal.

10. When the project has been completed, create a presentation for Slideshare and add it as a piece of Rich Media, encourage your project collaborators to do the same.

11. Add the details of the project to the *Projects* section of your profile and encourage your fellow collaborators to do the same.

MARKET YOUR BUSINESS

As I was often told, the world is full of amazing products gathering dust simply for lack of a sale. Without marketing, no one will know either you or your business exists. As much effort needs to be put into creating a marketing strategy as is put into product and service development and delivery.

The activities you need to engage in to market your business include:

- Understand who your target market is and why they might want to buy what you are selling.

- Decide which of the various groups you could sell to are your priority.

- Determine the most appropriate 'key message' they are likely to respond to.

To market your business on LinkedIn, you will need to:

1. Create a business profile on a LinkedIn company page.

2. Add a LinkedIn badge to your company website.

3. Update your personal profile to include details of specialities and the goals you have set for the company.

4. Encourage your staff to create engaging profiles that are kept updated. You could use a local photographer to take all the company photos.

5. Talk about what your business is doing in your personal and company status updates.

6. If you are hosting or taking part in any events, don't forget to include them as status updates, consider inviting named guests from your network.

7. Embed company presentations in Slideshare and share as Rich Media on your personal profile.

8. Upload public company presentations to your company page and share them with your followers.

9. Create links to company owned content, such as videos and presentations in personal and company status updates.

10. Add the company Twitter account to your LinkedIn profile to ensure any status updates you create are broadcast to your Twitter followers.

11. Join in discussions in relevant industry groups.

12. Ask for personal and company recommendations from clients you know are satisfied with the work you have done on their behalf.

13. Segment your connections into relevant groups through tags and then keep them informed about developments in your business.

MARKET YOUR WEBSITE

A website needs exposure as much as a business does in order to encourage people to come and have a look at what you are doing, the products and services you offer and to find out what distinguishes you from your competitors. There is much you can do to help yourself, but essentially, the tasks you will need to undertake are to:

- Be visible online. This includes adding your link to relevant directories, lists and industry specific websites.

- Ensure you are adding interesting information to your website on a regular basis as this will encourage visitors to come and read what you have to say.

- Make sure your website has a mechanism to capture information from the people interested in what you have to offer. This might be a subscription option or a simple form allowing people to get a brochure delivered.

On LinkedIn the tasks most effective at marketing your website are those which generate interest in what you have to say, and you should consider becoming active in at least some of the following areas:

1. Update your personal profile, and encourage other staff members to update theirs, to include links to your company website and/or blog.

2. Regularly post links to interesting material in your status updates.

3. Add the company Twitter account to your LinkedIn profile to ensure any status updates with website links in are broadcast to your Twitter followers as well.

4. Add a news item to your groups whenever you create a new article to your website

5. If you have a WordPress.com blog, use the publicize feature to send your blog posts to your status updates automatically.

6. Use the promotions section of groups to share links to information about any special offers, deals or events.

NETWORKING FOR SUCCESS

It is unlikely you would be active on LinkedIn if you weren't aware of just how powerful networking can be. However, that said, there is an art to networking which creates the difference between being successful and mediocre. Typically this is demonstrated by successful networkers who know the person they are 'talking' to; whether online or in the physical world, are usually not the people they are selling themselves to. The purpose of networking is to build a relationship formed out of trust. That trust will allow the people you have relationships with, to recommend you to their friends, colleagues and clients, safe in the knowledge you will deliver on the promises you make.

In this section, you will find three recipes to help you:

- Be recognised as an industry expert.

- Build your personal brand.

- Create an engaging headline.

BECOME AN INDUSTRY EXPERT

What exactly is an Industry expert? To my mind these are the people to whom I would go if I had a question I couldn't answer, because I know they have more experience than I do. Even if they can't answer the question directly, they will almost certainly know where to look for the answer. They are usually people who like to help others and who aren't worried about keeping the knowledge they have secret.

There are three ways to become an industry expert:

- To write about what you know in journals, magazines and periodicals.

- To make presentations to groups about the market sector you work in.

- To answer questions and join in discussions in groups.

LinkedIn allows you to do all of these activities in a highly visible way, and the actions may include the following.

1. Develop your profile to demonstrate and qualify why you are able to talk with authority about the subjects you are interested in. This includes adding relevant experience, qualifications, courses and publications.

2. Take part in discussions in relevant groups and where appropriate share links to things you have written to back up the opinion you are sharing.

3. Answer questions other people have posed, in groups you are a member of, about the subjects you are knowledgeable about.

4. Add links to articles you have published or books you have written as news items in your groups.

111

5. Use status updates to post links to content you create and share online.

6. Ask for, and accept, recommendations from contacts you have worked with. You may also wish to ask for them in a specific format.

7. Include speaking engagements, presentations you are making and events you are presenting at in your status updates.

8. Share rich media content on your profile in the form of white papers, presentations, speeches and videos.

9. Select the right skills for people to endorse on your behalf.

10. Share content from thought leaders and connections you have found helpful and valuable.

BUILD BRAND 'YOU'

Personal branding is all the rage now and it involves creating an image of you that is both appropriate and sustainable. It works on the premise we will all have many different roles over the course of a lifetime; each one of those roles informs the person we are at the present time. This work involves ensuring our public persona is the one we wish to promote at any given time and requires the following actions to be undertaken on a regular basis:

- Having an up to date profile.

- Consistently developing a network of people who know you and what you do.

- Be visible within your network and to the people you want to get to know.

LinkedIn is the perfect place to begin building a personal brand, and the activities that will be most helpful include:

1. Ensuring your profile is filled out completely, this includes past positions as well as your education and a photograph.

2. Keeping your profile updated with any changes, including your contact details.

3. Creating a custom URL you can use on a business card, email signature or in other promotional literature.

4. Writing an eye-catching headline encouraging people to read your profile.

5. Regularly adding connections to your LinkedIn profile, particularly those people you have met and who are influential within your industry.

6. Using the skills and expertise and summary section of your profile to add specific keywords for the work you do.

7. Aiming to get in touch with at least one person you are already connected to every work day, even if it's just to say hello.

8. Including all your contact details in your profile, especially your email address.

9. Changing your settings to show the maximum visible profile to the search engines.

10. Sharing specific content you come across with individual contacts who might be interested.

11. Endorsing and asking to be endorsed by members of your network

12. Thank those who have endorsed you, connected with you, shared your updates, liked your content and sent you recommendations.

CREATE AN ENGAGING HEADLINE

An interesting and engaging headline is what helps people to decide whether or not they are going to read more about you when they find you through a LinkedIn search or group member list.

Your headline needs to summarise in one line who you are, what you do and what makes you stand out from the crowd. My current headline reads "Best Selling Author of LinkedIn Made Easy; Social Media Coach, Trainer & Strategist; Social Entrepreneur & Blogger". It says exactly what I do and gives me a way of asserting authority about the things I talk about on LinkedIn. In fact, I use similar headlines in many different places online.

If you want to be seen by the people who matter on LinkedIn then the following is a list of the actions you could consider taking.

1. Your headline will be set automatically to the job you listed as your current or most recent, this needs to be changed.

2. Search for and read the headlines of other people in your industry on LinkedIn to get ideas about keywords and structure.

3. Ask your clients what makes you stand out from your competitors.

4. Include your specialities or location (if this is important).

5. Use the search facility to find the people who are most connected within your industry to see what they say about themselves.

6. Include a good head and shoulders photograph, this is often shown in conjunction with your headline, and plays a key part in whether people remember meeting you or not.

RESEARCH AND DEVELOPMENT

All businesses, whatever their size and nature, are built upon the products and/or services they sell to their customers and clients. It is also true to say products come and go, they change according to politics, fashion and the media. Who, for instance, could have predicted the massive impact on every aspect of our lives the Internet or mobile phones would have back in the 1980's.

In order to keep up with the pace of change, we need to undertake a huge amount of research and development, not only about products and services, but also skill sets as new jobs come into being to reflect the change that happens.

In this section, you will find recipes to help you:

- Research new products and services.

- Find the right people for your job.

- Ensure your knowledge and understanding reflects the latest trends and changes.

RESEARCH PRODUCTS AND SERVICES

Having products to sell and services to offer are the lifeblood of any business, without these core components you don't actually have a business. And yet, these can change according to the season, global events and developments in technology.

Now we all have digital cameras there is no need for the photographic print shop which used to take a roll of film, and provide us with a neat envelope containing 24 or 36 fixed size photographs to show to friends and relatives. All of a sudden we were able to take the photograph and print it ourselves or share it on Flickr and Pintrest. This change in technology meant the industry had to adapt quickly or lose out altogether.

We are also bombarded daily with information, data and reports; it seems we can hardly move for the avalanche of email landing in our inbox. So how do you balance the need to know what is going on in your industry with the need to do the work?

LinkedIn allows you to keep up to date with your market sector quickly and easily and to do so you will need to take the following actions:

1. Join relevant industry groups and take part in discussions.

2. Make sure your group settings are set to receive Group Updates as a daily or weekly digest.

3. Seek out key players in your industry sector and if you can, follow their updates.

4. Create saved searches on LinkedIn for industry keywords and terminology.

5. Read the most recent and relevant presentations from those who are important in your market sector by finding them on their profile.

6. Use the Polls feature in groups to create quick overviews of an issue.

7. Find relevant industry blogs, which are updated regularly by scanning your contacts profiles.

8. Follow the Influencers for your Industry sector and follow relevant industry news feeds through LinkedIn Today.

9. Identify relevant companies and follow their updates.

10. Search for people on LinkedIn who have listed Patents or Patents Pending in their profiles. This could give you some great ideas for people to connect with and ideas for the future.

11. Search LinkedIn Companies for specific products and services you may be interested in.

FIND EMPLOYEES

Most businesses would list their people as their most valuable asset and it goes without saying for this to be the case, they need people who have the right combination of skill, attitude and knowledge in order to be successful.

Yet, recruitment is an area often fraught with complications and potential problems. To ensure you have the right people in the right place at the right time a business would normally need to undertake the following activities:

- Advertise a job as being available.

- Accept and vet applications.

- Interview and appoint the right client.

Although LinkedIn can do many things, one thing it can't do is the actual interview of an applicant. But, it can do a lot to help ensure you are talking to the right people in the first place. In order to do that you will need to do the following actions:

1. Investigate the current role descriptions being used for a particular position by finding similar jobs through the job search function of the site.

2. Post your job in the jobs section of LinkedIn (this does have a cost attached to it).

3. Add your job to the jobs section of any relevant industry groups you are a member of.

4. Contact your network to see if they have any recommendations of people who might be appropriate.

5. Consider doing a search for current industry professionals who have the right skill set and make them a direct approach.

6. Use LinkedIn when you receive applications to check profiles and reference information.

7. Use LinkedIn as a resource to target the right questions for interviews. You could ask them about their current or past roles, or what they think of a subject you know they have answered a question on.

8. Looking up their contacts will give you a good idea of their network and how active they are in a specific market sector.

9. Add a request to your company page together with a link to more information about the job you have available.

CONTINUING PROFESSIONAL DEVELOPMENT

Undertaking continuing professional development (CPD) is usually a requirement of on-going membership of a professional body and in many cases it involves attendance at key events, training courses and the successful completion of exams and relevant certification. Increasingly though, the professional bodies are also taking into account online activity as a sign of continuing competency to practice, at least for a part of the CPD requirement.

There are a number of ways in which LinkedIn can help you keep your knowledge and understanding up to date and they include:

1. Being an active part of the LinkedIn community, sharing status updates and other information.

2. Contributing to discussions in the professional Groups you belong to.

3. Joining University and College alumni groups, especially if there are industry sub groups attached to them.

4. Using the members list in your groups to find people you can add to your contact list

5. Creating industry tags for your connections, allowing you to keep up to date with specific groups of people you are connected to.

6. Adding tags to your network members so you can find specific sets of skills and interests at a later date.

7. Using the 'follow' feature to keep up to date with your industry influencers.

8. Ensure your profile has the relevant certifications sections added, keep this up to date to demonstrate compliance.

JOB HUNTING

The focus of this book has been on supporting the business use of LinkedIn and yet, there are more people using LinkedIn who are employed than are running their own company. Many of the former group of people will change their job, their role even their whole career several times in the course of a lifetime.

This group of recipes is for the person looking for new job and career opportunities and covers the following areas:

- Finding a job.

- Creating a brilliant portfolio.

- Finding a potential employer.

FIND A JOB

Let's say you are an accountant and your partner has been offered a job in another part of the country. What will you do to accommodate their career development? Will you move with them and if so, will you be looking for another position as an accountant or even take the opportunity to go in a completely different direction?

Finding a new job is quite a daunting prospect for many people. In much the same way employers have to take new recruits on blind faith that their resume and interview have given them the tools to be certain they will fit in; new employees will hope the post they have just accepted will give them the opportunity to develop their career further, in an environment that is both supportive and challenging.

So how can LinkedIn ensure you find the perfect new position, well if you do undertake the following activities, you will at least put yourself in a good starting place:

1. Ensure your profile is complete and up to date with details of any past and current roles, specific responsibilities and goals.

2. Add in relevant additional sections such as projects, courses and certifications, where necessary.

3. Don't forget to list any achievements to date, especially those which demonstrate you are able to deliver on targets.

4. Join relevant industry groups and monitor the job board within them to see if anything appropriate is announced.

5. Use the advanced job search to find posts in specific locations, levels and industries.

6. Make a list of the current keywords that might be used to define the role you are looking for. For example, SEO and search engine optimisation mean the same thing. You will minimise the potential for missing great jobs simply because you are looking for different terminology.

7. Once you have found a possible job, research the company through their Company page (if they have one).

8. Find out if anyone you are connected to is, or was, employed by the same company. They may be able to fill you in on company details.

9. List your skills and encourage your network to endorse you.

10. Identify people in your network you could speak to about developing your career in different directions.

11. Make sure you have a great covering letter ready in a text file so you can simply copy and paste it into this section of the online application form. Don't forget to address this personally to the person who posted the job advert.

CREATE A BRILLIANT PORTFOLIO

For portfolio, read resume, CV or profile; one or more of these will be needed to apply for any position advertised, wherever it may be. This is the one piece of information a future employer will judge you most harshly on and it needs to be the right information, presented in the best way to illustrate your suitability for the role you are applying for.

Your portfolio will also be used to help demonstrate three things:

- Your skill set and levels of expertise are appropriate.

- You have experience.

- You are the type of person who will fit into an existing team.

LinkedIn will help you to do all of these activities and more if you use it to its fullest potential with the following actions:

1. Ensure your profile is up to date, accurate and complete. Add a current photograph too.

2. Create an engaging and interesting headline to help differentiate you and demonstrate your understanding of industry needs.

3. Consider adding links to any personal websites or blogs, especially if they are relevant to your area of expertise.

4. Add presentations, videos, white papers and images you have created in the Summary, Experience and Education sections of your profile (consider copyright issues and check with your current employer before uploading, if you created them on their behalf).

5. Be active in groups, especially those containing key players in the companies you might like to work with.

6. Respond to any questions asked in groups you belong to, especially where it can showcase your knowledge and expertise.

FIND A NEW EMPLOYER

Although this is similar, it's not quite the same as finding a job. This requires a different tactic and outside of LinkedIn, would probably be undertaken by sending speculative letters and emails to potential employers to find out if there were any opportunities available.

However, within LinkedIn we can employ some slightly different tricks which may have a greater chance of success in the longer term; this can be a long game, so be prepared to work at it for some time before getting a result.

The actions you could take to be successful include:

1. Research which companies use the skills you offer and then filter them to find the ones right for you. This might be based on location, size, market sector or profile.

2. Research the employee list through the company's page to find out whether there are any particular considerations around company values, ethics and culture you need to take account of.

3. Using the employee list, find out if there is anyone you're directly connected to and get in touch to find out if they can point you to the right person to engage with.

4. Ask your network of contacts if anyone can introduce you to the company, especially one or more of the people who might be responsible for recruitment in your particular area of interest.

5. Once you have found the right person to contact, try to join the same groups, participate in the same discussions and answer the questions they have either asked or answered. Follow their status

updates, comment on them and share them where appropriate (of course, overuse of this could be seen as stalking!).

6. Ask a question yourself and if someone at the company responds, ask them to connect with you, they can only say 'no'.

7. Use your status updates as a way of advertising your interest in a particular company; if they are paying attention then it is possible they could pick it up.

USEFUL RESOURCES

There are many resources you might find useful that will help you use LinkedIn even more effectively, and I have listed just a few of the ones I can be sure won't change to help you.

LinkedIn Help Center

This has to be the first port of call if you have a question not seeming to be answered anywhere else. You can find it at: *help.linkedin.com*.

LinkedIn Blog

The LinkedIn Blog will keep you up to date with the latest news and updates on the network, it's at: *blog.LinkedIn.com*.

Official LinkedIn YouTube Channel

There are a huge number of videos walking you through what LinkedIn is and how to use it at: *youtube.com/user/LinkedIn*.

LinkedIn on Twitter

Everyone seems to be on Twitter these days and if you want to keep up with what's happening with LinkedIn then you can follow their tweets at: *Twitter.com/LinkedIn*.

Personal Branding: If you want to know more about Personal Branding in general, then I suggest you check out Dan Scwabel's blog at *personalbrandingblog.com*.

USEFUL NETWORKING BOOKS

Much of what I've talked about in this book, aside from the specifics about how to do something in particular, looks at what makes a person effective on LinkedIn; mostly these skills are related to networking in the broader sense and I wanted to list a few books here I have found useful over the last couple of years. They have helped me to hone my own networking skills and given me helpful hints and tips I have taken on to the social networks, and primarily onto LinkedIn itself.

... and death came third - Andy Lopata and Peter Roper

Click, What we do online and why - Bill Tancer

Flip - Peter Sheahan

Networking for Success - Carol Roper

Rain Making - Ford Harding

Recommended - Andy Lopata

The Jelly Effect - Andy Bounds

The Tipping Point - Malcolm Gladwell

Truth or Delusion - Ivan Misner

REFERENCES

1.   The Future of LinkedIn and the Economic Graph -
     10/12/12 - LinkedIn Today.

2.   Social Proof Theory:
     http://en.wikipedia.org/wiki/Social_proof.

3.   Harding F. Rain Making: Attract New Clients No Matter
     What Your Field; 2008; Adams Media.

4.   http://www.edge.org/3rd_culture/christakis_fowler08/
     christakis_fowler08_index.html

5.   http://learn.linkedin.com/job-seekers.

ABOUT THE AUTHOR

Linda Parkinson-Hardman is the author of six other non-fiction books plus one short story. She is also the Founder and CEO of The Hysterectomy Association, and the LinkedIn and Social Media Specialist for Internet Mentor Dorset Limited.

Her job is to remove the mystique and fear from social media. She works as a social media strategist, coach and trainer providing organisations, businesses and individual clients with bespoke solutions that help them to utilise the networks more effectively.

As a social entrepreneur, she founded the Hysterectomy Association in 1997. It has supported millions of women over the years with impartial, appropriate information through a huge network of thousands of women all helping each other. If you'd like to meet her, you can often find her lurking at conferences, seminars and presentations either on or off the stage.

She lives in rural West Dorset with her partner Steve Graham and has no kids, dogs or cats and has no plans to acquire any either.

You can connect with Linda on the social web on:

LinkedIn: http://www.linkedin.com/in/lindaph

Blog: http://womanontheedgeofreality.com

Twitter: http://www.Twitter.com/lindaph

Facebook: www.facebook.com/LindaParkinsonHardman

Slideshare: http://www.slideshare.net/lindaph1

YouTube: http://www.youtube.com/user/lindaphardman

Also by Linda Parkinson-Hardman

How to Build a Brilliant Business with the Internet: 101 essential hints & tips for every successful small business & entrepreneur.

Broadcasting Powerful Messages with Twitter.

101 Handy Hints for a Happy Hysterectomy.

Losing the Woman Within.

The Pocket Guide to Hysterectomy.

Woman on the Edge of Reality - Novel

A Diva's Guide to the Menopause - Short Story.

5972570R00088

Printed in Great Britain
by Amazon.co.uk, Ltd.,
Marston Gate.